NeuroSuccess
Your Brain Retraining Guide to Wealth and Accomplishment

by Edward Hughes

Dear Esteemed Reader,

Thank you immensely for choosing this book to join your collection. We imagine that you've already embarked on an exploration of ideas within these pages, and we couldn't be happier about it!

Now, if you find yourself chuckling, pondering, or even debating with the words in front of you, we'd absolutely love to hear about it. If you can spare a few moments to pen down your thoughts in a review, we would be as delighted as a dictionary on a spelling bee!

An Amazon review would be excellent - but hey, we're far from picky. Whether it's a scribble on the back of a grocery list, a tweet, or even a message in a bottle (though that might take a while to reach us), your feedback is gold.

Writing a review might not be as fun as a spontaneous dance-off, but we promise it'll bring grins to our faces, warmth to our hearts, and incredibly valuable insights to future readers.

With Gratitude,

Bo Bennett, PhD
Publisher
Archieboy Holdings, LLC.

Table of Contents

Introduction

Success is not a serendipity, nor is it an elusive aspiration reserved solely for the fortunate few. It is, in fact, a byproduct of a system of mental training and transformations. At its core, it stems from a profound understanding of how our most potent tool - the brain - functions. This book is a comprehensive guide, aimed at unveiling the untapped potential of your mind, focusing primarily on 'NeuroSuccess'. It is designed to help you understand, utilize, and teach your brain to be more driven and result-oriented.

'NeuroSuccess' implies harnessing the power of your brain to manifest continual success in your life- whether it's career growth, fulfilling relationships, or personal accomplishment. Our brain is an adaptable marvel, constantly evolving and adapting to stimuli. Recognizing its power can be your stepping stone to rewiring patterns of thought, breaking-free from the shackles of limiting beliefs, and manifesting success as smooth and frequent as your next breath. This isn't just theoretical fluff; it's a tested and proven concept backed by cutting edge neuroscience research and real-life testimonials.

With a blend of actionable advice, backed by science, you'll dive deep into various facets of your brain and life, each chapter spanned across various themes - understanding your brain, foundations of success, mastering procrastination, leveraging emotions, among others. Each shares the common thread of NeuroSuccess, inching you closer towards the goals you aspire to achieve. However, ingesting information is just one part of the equation; the implementation will be on you. Are you prepared and willing to condition your brain towards constant success? If 'yes', turn the page and begin the journey of self-discovery and transformation.

The Power of the Brain: An Overview

The human brain is an organ of such extraordinary complexity that it's often compared to the universe itself. Despite its humble size, it's the ultimate command center for our body, the hold space for our consciousness, our notions of self, and our place in the world.

The brain is our greatest natural resource, responsible for all the achievements of the human race. Behind every scientific discovery, every work of art, every heartfelt connection, and every journey we embark on, it's this three-pound organ working ceaselessly, quietly in the dark of our skulls. It's responsible for our ideas, values, emotions, memories, perceptions, and the intricate ballet of movements we call life.

Yet, despite its pivotal role in our existence, many of us tend to undervalue its significance. At school, we learn about the importance of a healthy heart, lungs, and muscles, but when was the last time someone emphasized the power of a healthy, disciplined mind? The fact remains that as much as we need a strong body, we need an even stronger mind to achieve success in all realms of life. This realization brings us to a fundamental understanding - the mind is the powerhouse that fuels our journey to success.

The brain is constantly evolving, building connections, and pruning away less-used pathways in response to our experiences and emotions. This constant change, known as brain plasticity, is at the root of our capacity adapt, learn, and grow. This adaptability, when harnessed and directed, has the potential to lead us to unparalleled heights of achievement and success.

If the brain is the main command center for our success, it only makes sense to learn how to optimize its performance. Understanding the brain and its workings is not just important for neuroscientists, but for all individuals eager to unlock their full potential. The ability to rewire our brain for success, a concept we will delve into in this book, is a powerful tool that can drastically transform not just our personal and professional lives, but our overall view of the world.

Imagine your mind as the most powerful computer on Earth, whose programming determines your outlook on life, productivity, relationships, and ultimately success. Most of us are running on outdated software, not because we aren't capable of upgrading, but because we're unaware. But what if you could update it? Imagine reprogramming your mind to optimize productivity, enhance creativity, improve decision-making, and cultivate resilience against stress and adversity. That's the power we have at our disposal with knowledge and training of the brain.

The concept of NeuroSuccess, introduced in this book, is about leveraging the science of neuroplasticity for success. It's about gaining a clear understanding of how our brain works, and using that knowledge to cultivate cognitive and emotional traits associated with success. This approach empowers us to take control of our mental programming, and ultimately, our destiny.

Success seems elusive to many because they focus exclusively on external conditions, when the key to achievement lies within. Our brain actively interprets, constructs, and narrates our life experiences. If we can guide this process in a positive, beneficial way, we can lead ourselves to an enriching path of success.

Yet, the process isn't as simple as flipping a switch. Just as building physical strength requires time, effort, and steady discipline, enhancing brain power demands consistent training and patience. Our brain is a muscle that can strengthen with the right exercises and weaken with neglect. However, the rewards of dedication and commitment towards brain training are immeasurable, extending far beyond the attainment of material wealth to include emotional resilience, relationship satisfaction, and genuine happiness.

It's important to shed the misconception that our brains are rigid and unchangeable. Scientific research supports the opposite. Our brains remain plastic, or moldable, throughout our lifetime. This means our habits, skills, thought patterns, and beliefs aren't concrete. With effort, we can change them, to align with our vision of success.

The road to NeuroSuccess isn't without challenges. Old habits can be stubborn, doubts may creep in, and there may be moments of failure. Nevertheless, the transformative potential of a consciously guided mind can overcome these hurdles. In this book, we'll be providing you with strategies and techniques to navigate these obstacles effectively.

The journey towards NeuroSuccess begins with a single step - understanding the power of your brain. As you explore the following chapters and uncover fascinating insights about your brain, remember the words of Henry Ford, "Whether you think you can or think you can't, you're right." Your mindset, shaped by your brain, holds the key to your success.

Embrace this journey with an open mind, and let the transformative power of your brain guide you towards the success you seek. Remember, true change begins from the inside, and there's no tool more potent than your brain to drive this transformation. Harness your brain's extraordinary capability, and unlock the success you're undoubtedly capable of achieving.

The power doesn't lie outside of you, but within you, in the incredible organ that is your brain. Ready for the journey? Let's delve deeper into the world of NeuroSuccess.

Why NeuroSuccess?

Following a journey of self-improvement, which had its rudiments in understanding the power of the brain, we're now ready to delve into the "why" of NeuroSuccess. On the surface, NeuroSuccess may appear similar to other self-help tools. However, the unique approach rooted in neuroscience sets this method apart.

To put it simply, NeuroSuccess is about harnessing the full potential of your brain. It's about overthrowing traditional, often flawed methodologies of working harder and turning to a smarter way of accomplishing your goals. It all comes down to training your brain, reshaping your mindset, and tapping into the limitless potential that lies within our neural networks.

Our brain is a powerful engine that governs everything we say, do, or feel. By understanding how it works, we can create an actionable roadmap towards success. We aren't talking just about ephemeral victories but lasting, significant achievements that result in serious life transformation.

NeuroSuccess empowers you to truly control your life instead of being a puppet to random circumstances. It equips you with the understanding and tools to take control of your cognitive processes, guide your thoughts and emotions, and shape the path towards your desired future.

The essence of NeuroSuccess lies not just in understanding your brain but learning how to use this knowledge intelligibly. The first step to success starts with understanding that you have more power over your life than you think. It's about consciously being in command of your actions instead of reacting mindlessly to external stimuli.

Scientific advancements have helped us understand that our brain changes throughout our lifetime, and, intriguingly, we can influence these changes. As we gain new experiences, our neurons forge new connections while old, less useful ones fade away. This phenomenon is known as neuroplasticity. NeuroSuccess leverages this concept to adapt and evolve our brains according to our ambitions.

Often, the path to success looks daunting due to perceived barriers. Among these barriers are self-defeating mindsets, negative constructs, procrastination, fear, and doubt. The good news is that with the help of NeuroSuccess, we can overcome these obstacles. By rewiring our neural networks, we can remove these impediments and cultivate a brain built for success.

NeuroSuccess also reconciles the importance of both intrinsic and extrinsic motivation. We all need the drive to act, and this push often comes from rewards we seek or the satisfaction we feel from performing an act. By reshaping our neural pathways, we're better suited to find motivation consistently, thereby improving our overall productivity and pleasure in life.

A significant component of NeuroSuccess involves building successful habits. Success, after all, is not a one-time event but a consistent pattern. In that respect, forming successful habits translates directly into long-term success. By understanding the science of habit formation and neural reprogramming, we help enact enduring positive changes to our behavior.

Yet another vital aspect of NeuroSuccess is emotional intelligence. Emotions play a crucial role in our life, dictating our responses to different situations. By understanding their influence and learning to regulate them, we can respond effectively to various scenarios, personal or professional, leading to better outcomes in life.

Brain health also figures prominently in NeuroSuccess. A healthy brain functions with optimal efficiency, contributing directly to overall cognitive function enhancement, which, in turn, improves our chances of success. By adopting a neuro-friendly lifestyle including good nutrition, regular exercise, and adequate sleep, we can maintain our brains in peak performance condition.

NeuroSuccess is not about quick fixes or short-term solutions. It is a lifelong commitment to continually investing in your brain health and cognitive function. Your brain carries an immense transformation potential. By making NeuroSuccess a part of your life, you're choosing a scientifically-grounded, effective method for personal development and lifelong success.

In summary, we embrace NeuroSuccess because it is an evidence-based, concrete approach to success. Unlike other self-help strategies rooted in vagueness, NeuroSuccess directly addresses the engine behind it all, the brain. By understanding and harnessing its immense potential, we gain a direct route to professional accomplishment, personal growth, and overall life satisfaction.

15

Chapter 1: Understanding Your Brain

As we delve into the intricacies of the human brain and its potential, you'll find that it's less of an enigma than you might have imagined. Yes, your brain is fabulously complex, comprised of billions of neurons interconnected in networks that allow you to think, emote, and act. At the very core of it lie these neurons, the basic units that transmit signals, creating a symphony of neural communication that, quite literally, makes you, you. However, this orchestra isn't fixed - it's plastic. Not like your coffee lid, but in the sense that it can morph, grow, and adapt, a phenomenon known as brain plasticity. This adaptability allows your brain to evolve based on experiences, helping you learn and adjust. Moreover, we can categorize the brain into three main components, often referred to as the triune brain: the reptilian brain (instinct), the limbic system (emotion), and the neocortex (rational thought). Each part plays a distinct role in governing how you respond to the world around you, with instinctual survival impulses often clashing with rational thought. Understanding your brain isn't as simple as labeling parts and functions. It's about appreciating the fluid interplay of these elements, recognizing its potential for growth and change, to begin the journey towards self-evolution and success.

Neurons and Networks: The Basic Units

The primary unit of the neural structure, where the phenomenal power of your brain begins, can be found at the cellular level: Neurons. These special cells form the unshakeable foundation of your brain's mighty capacities. Now, you might have a basic understanding of them, but let's get into this a little deeper.

A neuron, simply put, is a nerve cell. It's intended to transport information. Your brain carries millions of these cells and they are the messengers. A neuron communicates via electricity and chemicals, from within your brain to the farthest reaches of your body. This fundamental unit holds the potential to store an immense amount of memory and enables you to learn and adapt. Thus, even seemingly simple actions like lifting a finger or remembering a name, include a multitude of neuronic conversations.

The second primary unit, just as crucial as the neuron, is the Neural Network. "Network?" you may ask. Exactly! Your neurons are not lone rangers; they exist within an intricate web, continually interacting with each other within this network. Multiple neurons converging form these networks or 'neural pathways' and these pathways are the building blocks of habits, learning, and memory.

Each and every experience you encounter triggers the development of a unique neural pathway. These pathways are constantly changing and evolving. If a certain pathway is used frequently, it becomes stronger and more established. This is how habits, both beneficial and detrimental, take form. On the contrary, rarely used pathways can weaken and eventually disappear. This powerful property of the brain, known as neuroplasticity, is our brain's way of continually adapting to our environment, a topic we will delve into further in the next section.

A neural network operates by transmitting signals. Every time a neuron fires, it recounts the neural message, called an action potential, down the line to the next neuron. This propagation takes place via the synapse, a minute space separating two neurons. The process is facilitated by neurotransmitters, chemical messengers that 'jump the gap' and convey the message from one neuron to another.

One key concept that amplifies the function of neurons and neural networks is the 'neural firing threshold.' This threshold permits a neuron to ascertain whether the incoming signal is potent enough to be transmitted further. If the incoming signal does not 'trigger the threshold,' the neuron remains inactive and the signal is terminated. However, when the signal strength surpasses the neuron's threshold, the message is carried on through the network, leading to thought processes, feelings, and consequent actions.

The strength and resilience of these neuron networks are not merely intrinsic – they're moldable. The creation and strengthening of neural pathways are driven by two rules: 'Neurons that fire together, wire together' and 'Use it or lose it.' When certain neurons frequently fire together, the connection between them grows stronger, hence forging more robust networks. Conversely, the less frequently neurons fire together, the connection grows weaker. This process is a part of the foundation for learning new skills and habits.

Let's consider the connection with success. Each successful experience, every win, each moment of accomplishment, equips you with a unique set of neural pathways that become associated with success. The repetitive activation of these 'success networks' gradually accustoms your brain to a success-oriented paradigm, thereby rewiring your brain for continual achievements.

However, it's important to recognize that the same principal applies to failure as well. Negative experiences also create their neural pathways, and repetition of these incidents can reinforce a 'failure mindset'. But don't worry, all is not lost! Just as the brain can be wired for failure, it can also be rewired for success. With intentional thought patterns and specific activities (more on that in subsequent chapters), these harmful networks can be weakened and the beneficial ones strengthened.

As you start gaining an understanding of these basic units of the brain, their functionality, and influence on our daily life including habits, skills, and mindset, you'll realize that your success is far from being an abstract concept. It's wired into the very structure of your brain. It's about how you perceive and respond to the various situations of life, and how your neurons and networks propagate these responses.

To wrap this up, a wise way to think about neurons and networks is this: The neuron is a concept, an idea, or a thought, and the neural network is the story. And just like any good story, it can be rewritten. Your aims, ambitions, and actions all contribute to the grand narrative of your own success. The understanding and mastery of these basic units could, indeed, provide a fresh trajectory towards your personal and professional milestones.

With this foundational understanding, let's journey to the next phase in understanding our mighty brain- 'The Brain's Plasticity: Adapting and Evolving'. Remember, you're not merely a product of your brain's wirings, rather, you are its architect. Utilizing the power of neurons and neural networks strategically could potentially lead to lifetimes of success and achievement.

The Brain's Plasticity: Adapting and Evolving

As we carry on our journey of understanding the incredible power of the brain, we come to a concept called 'neuroplasticity'. This complex term encapsulates a relatively simple idea; our brains are, to a degree, malleable and adaptable. They're capable of learning, growing, and changing course based on new experiences, behaviors, and thoughts.

First, let's look at what we mean by 'plasticity'. In the realm of neuroscience, plasticity refers to the brain's capacity to change and adapt on a physical level in response to stimulation from the environment. These changes manifest in alterations to the brain's structure, function, and organization.

It was once believed that the brain could only change during critical periods in early childhood, with the neural pathways more or less fixed as we age. However, an abundance of evidence over the last few decades has proven this view to be outdated. The brain, we've discovered, retains plasticity throughout our lives.

This lifelong plasticity allows us to learn new skills, adapt to new environments, and even recover from brain injuries. Importantly, it also means that through conscious effort, we can change our brain to become more successful, more productive, and more fulfilled in whatever field or endeavor we pursue.

At its heart, neuroplasticity operates on a 'use it or lose it' principle. The more you use a particular neural pathway, whether it's for playing a musical instrument, mastering a new language, or cultivating a positive mindset, the stronger and more efficient that pathway becomes. And conversely, neural pathways that aren't used tend to weaken over time.

Neuroplasticity links directly to experience and learning, which occur when certain neural pathways strengthen while others weaken. Think of your brain as a vibrant, bustling city. The frequently travelled routes — the major highways and busy streets — become wider and faster to commute, while less-travelled paths grow over and deteriorate from lack of use.

The implications of neuroplasticity for personal development and success are staggering. It means that our thoughts, our behaviors, and our experiences quite literally shape our brains. This principle can be leveraged to cultivate a mindset primed for achievement.

Let's say you often engage in self-defeating thoughts, like "I'm not good enough" or "I'm destined to fail." Your brain, in its adaptability, has built strong, efficient neural pathways to accommodate these thoughts. But while the brain is adaptable, it's not judgmental. It responds just the same to positive thoughts and expectations. So by consciously and consistently steering your thoughts towards the positive — towards success, confidence, and fulfillment — you can foster new, empowering neural pathways.

But rewiring your brain for success isn't just about replacing negative thoughts with positive ones. It's also about cultivating the neural pathways that house your skills, talents, and discipline by regularly engaging in activities that stimulate them. If you're dedicated to becoming an accomplished writer, it means writing every day, even when you don't feel like it. It's reinforcing, strengthening, and optimizing your brain's writing 'highways'.

Neuroplasticity isn't a quick fix. Changing your brain takes time and consistent effort. And because the brain prioritizes frequently used neural pathways, overcoming deeply ingrained negative thought patterns or maladaptive behaviors can be challenging. But with understanding and persistence, science says you can do it.

One last point to remember — neuroplasticity is a double-edged sword. While it enables learning and growth, it also means that bad habits and unhelpful thought patterns can become deeply ingrained in the brain's structure. That's why it's so important to engage in regular positive habits and mindful self-reflection to ensure you're shaping your brain in the way you want.

Grasping this concept of neuroplasticity, the adaptability and evolution of our brains, is foundational in the progressive journey towards NeuroSuccess. With this in mind, you're better equipped to shape your brain, and as such, your life, into whatever form resonates with your vision of success. We have the power within us to change, to adapt, and to overcome- the power of neuroplasticity.

The Triune Brain: Instinct, Emotion, and Rational Thought

As we dive deeper into understanding the brain, we're now going to explore an influential theory known as the Triune Brain model. This vital and interesting concept helps us comprehend how different areas in our brains influence our behavior and thinking. It suggests that our brain is divided into three distinct parts—the reptilian complex (instinct), the limbic system (emotion), and the neocortex (rational thought).

The most basic level of our brain, in the terms of its development, is the reptilian complex. This is the part of our brain that's responsible for our survival instincts. When you feel the need to eat, sleep, or are startled by a sudden noise, that's the reptilian brain at work. It's pretty much set in stone in terms of its functionalities—it controls things that we can't alter through thought alone.

This 'reptilian' portion of the brain is both our strength and weakness. On one hand, it maintains essential automatic functions such as our heartbeat and body temperature. On the other, it is susceptible to reactive, unthinking behavior which, without the damping influence of the other brain structures, can lead to troublesome, or even harmful, actions.

Then we move to the limbic system, which governs our emotions. It's key to forming memories and is significantly involved in our experiences of pleasure, pain, and survival. Unlike the reptilian brain, the limbic system is influenced by learned experiences. That's why certain songs or smells can trigger powerful emotional memories. This part of the brain plays a crucial role in our behavior, shaping our responses based on emotion over instinct.

A healthy limbic system supports us in building gratifying, meaningful connections with others. However, when it's off-balance, it can lead to emotional upheaval and irrational behavior. For example, when we let our anger or fear dictate our action, it's usually because our limbic system is getting the upper hand over our more rational brain structures.

Lastly, we have the neocortex, the crowning glory of the human brain, this is where rational thought and complex decision-making take place. Humans have the most developed neocortex compared to other species. This is why we're capable of philosophical thinking, long-term planning, and other advanced cognitive abilities. The neocortex is where creativity blooms, and new ideas are formed.

At its best, our neocortex offers us the milestone of self-awareness and the ability to think and plan for the future. It keeps our instincts and emotions in check, and allows us to act in balanced, mindful ways. However, if our neocortex is not fully engaged, we risk becoming too impulsive or overly emotional—swinging the pendulum to the opposite extremes without rational control.

Understanding the triune brain model helps us recognize the tug-of-war between our instinct, emotion, and rational thought processes. This understanding can lead to greater self-awareness and self-control. Furthermore, it's paramount for us to integrate all parts of our brain—instinctive, emotional, and rational—in our quest for success.

Just as a well-tuned car operates better when all its parts are functioning in harmony, so too does our brain. Understanding and connecting with each part of our brain allows for a more coherent, integral operation. If our instinctive, emotional, and rational sides are working in concert, we're better equipped to respond to life's challenges effectively.

Ahead, we'll delve into the fundamentals of true success. This means not merely accumulating material wealth, but achieving a sense of fulfillment and purpose. Applying the knowledge about our triune brain is the first step to fostering a mindset conducive to success and living a more harmonious, balanced life.

It's essential to appreciate that while these three parts of our brain have the ability to function independently, they're most powerful when they're allowed to collaborate. Everyone has a unique balance, some people might lean more towards their instinctual side, some might be more emotional, and some might be more rational. However, to operate at full capacity, it's vital to engage all three components.

Our journey towards a 'NeuroSuccess' isn't about suppressing our instinctual or emotional segments, but about permitting our rational mind to guide and coordinate with them. By doing so, we can steer ourselves to success, not impulsively or haphazardly, but intentionally and purposefully.

So, it's time to harness the power of your triune brain. As we proceed, keep in mind always that every action, thought, or feeling is a product of these parts of your brain working in tandem. Recognizing their roles, potential, and limitations lays the foundation for becoming the master of your mind, propelling you towards the success that you aspire to achieve.

With this newfound understanding of our triune brain, we're poised to delve into the defining qualities and fundamentals of true success. The intent isn't to mold ourselves into someone else's idea of success, but to carve our own path based on a keen self-understanding and purposeful action. This wouldn't just lead us to material wealth, but also towards emotional fulfillment and intrinsic growth.

Chapter 2: The Foundations of Success

Continuing from where we left off, we delve into the bedrock underpinning success. True success goes beyond material wealth, it encompasses personal satisfaction, fulfillment and happiness in all areas of life. Defining what this looks like for you is the first crucial step, and it forms the cornerstone for the journey ahead. But simply visualizing these ideals isn't enough, there's a crucial role that mindset plays in turning this vision into reality. Much like a gardener tending to their plants, we must cultivate a growth mindset that nurtures our ambitions and fosters resilience in the face of adversity. This mindset influences our actions and reactions, shaping the course of our endeavors. Alongside this, belief systems significantly influence the outcome of our endeavors. These are the ingrained patterns of thought that subconsciously guide our decisions and behaviors, serving as a light guiding us through the foggy path to our goals. Understanding and positively influencing these elements form the bedrock, the very foundation of achieving success.

Defining True Success: Beyond Material Wealth

Most often, success is measured in tangible terms- wealth, status, or affluence. However, this perspective of success is skewed and often misleading. It's also crucial to note that true success extends far beyond mere material accumulation. Before you delve deeper into the intricacies of NeuroSuccess, it's important to define what 'success' actually means in the broader, more holistic sense.

For many, the concept of true success encompasses personal growth, spiritual development, emotional intelligence, and a strong, meaningful network of relationships. It's more about personal fulfillment and less about financial prosperity. While material wealth may be a byproduct of success, it is not an inclusive definition.

Imagine you have all the money you'll ever need, but no time to spend with loved ones, no satisfaction from your job, and poor physical health due to constant stress. Is that really success? This chapter will challenge that limited conception and redefine success, not as an end goal, but an ongoing journey of self-discovery and growth.

To begin, think about what 'success' means to you. True success is highly personal and varies greatly from person to person. It may mean being a good parent, establishing a fulfilling career, maintaining a healthy lifestyle, or simply living a life filled with happiness and peace. It's essential to identify your own definition of success, rather than swallowing society's version whole cloth.

When you encounter setbacks or obstacles, this personal success definition can help you stay focused, resilient, and motivated. It guides your actions, shaping your decisions, both big and small. It's your personal compass, pointing you towards true north amid the chaotic sea of life's challenges.

One of the vital elements of true success is personal fulfillment. You achieve fulfillment when you spend your time and effort on the things that you value the most. It comes from pursuing growth in all facets of life, nurturing your physical, mental, emotional, and spiritual well-being.

Success also means achieving balance in life. Striking a healthy work-life balance can be challenging goals, but it is crucial to ensure that one aspect doesn't completely overshadow the others. Too much focus on career and wealth can often result in neglecting personal relationships and health, leading to a sense of dissatisfaction and stress.

Another key component of true success lies in the quality of your relationships. Close, trusting relationships with friends, family and colleagues not only provide emotional support but also contribute to a sense of purpose and belonging. An essential aspect of NeuroSuccess is understanding the neural basis of these social bonds and learning how to nurture them effectively.

A successful person has a growth mindset and is committed to lifelong learning. The mindset you adopt towards your abilities and potential largely determines your life's outcomes. People with a growth mindset perceive failure as an opportunity to learn, which leads to resilience and eventual success.

Contribution and service to others are also critical elements of success. Serving others and making a positive impact on your community gives you a sense of purpose and fulfillment that wealth or prestige can't match. It brings forth a sense of accomplishment, knowing that you've truly made a difference in people's lives.

Achieving true success also calls for emotional intelligence. It's not enough to be intellectually smart; successful people excel in understanding, managing, and using their emotions in positive ways. This emotional prowess aids in overcoming challenges, defusing conflicts, and fostering good relationships.

In conclusion, the definition of true success is expansive and goes beyond wealth and material possessions. It's about achieving personal fulfillment, maintaining relationships, fostering a growth mindset, making a difference, and nurturing emotional intelligence. Having millions in the bank account doesn't define success if you lack these elements.

By expanding your definition of success, you can aim for a more well-rounded, fulfilling life. While it's not wrong to pursue wealth, it shouldn't come at the expense of other areas of your life. Remember, true success isn't about achieving one specific thing, it's embracing personal growth across all aspects of life.

As you progress through the following chapters, keep this definition of success in mind. Use it as a guide to shape your thoughts, decisions, and actions as you harness the power of your brain and march towards your own version of true success.

The Role of Mindset in Achieving Success

The concept of mindset plays a critical role in achieving success, regardless of what that concept means to each of us. Our mindset essentially reflects our attitudes and beliefs that direct our behavior and decisions. If you're searching for the road to success, your mindset is the roadmap to guide you there. Yet, it also holds the power to pave the road with obstacles, if left unchecked.

Success is not purely a product of luck or innate talent. It's the culmination of an individual's mindset, effort, persistence, and resilience. Consequently, it's crucial to cultivate a mindset conducive to success, which we'll discuss in depth.

The Growth Mindset is the conviction that our intelligence, talents, and abilities can be developed through dedication, learning, and hard work. It's the understanding that failure isn't a reflection of our worth or potential, but rather a stepping-stone towards improvement and ultimately success. This mindset empowers us to persevere through adversity, embracing challenges as chances for personal and professional growth.

On the flip side, there's the Fixed Mindset, characterized by the belief that our abilities are static and unchangeable. This mindset instigates fear of failure, restraining us from venturing outside our comfort zones. You're more likely to give up after facing failure in a Fixed Mindset, viewing it as a testament of your inability rather than a growth opportunity.

The implications of these mindsets stretch far beyond our perceptions of failure or ability. They also influence our desire to learn and grow, our resilience in the face of adversity, our perception of effort, our receptiveness to criticism, and our ability to find inspiration in the success of others. Therefore, it's clear that a Growth Mindset is better suited for fostering success.

Now that we've distinguished between these two mindsets, how can we ensure we're cultivating a Growth Mindset? It begins with awareness. Becoming mindful of our thoughts and attitudes enables us to recognize when we're slipping into a Fixed Mindset. Acknowledge that capabilities aren't predetermined and can be honed and expanded with effort and time, and that failure isn't fatal but instructive.

Furthermore, changing one's language can be a powerful tool to cultivate a Growth Mindset. Instead of thinking "I can't do this," consider "What am I missing?" Rather than saying "This is too hard," try "This may take some time and effort." It's amazing how a slight tweak in your language can entirely change your approach and perspective.

Setting achievable goals is also central in fostering a Growth Mindset. If your targets are systematically unreachable, it may foster feelings of defeat and reverberate a Fixed Mindset. Conversely, measurable and reasonable goals can fuel a sense of accomplishment, promoting resilience and furthering your Growth Mindset.

We should also highlight the importance of mentorship and guidance in establishing a Growth Mindset. Mentors can provide valuable insights, support, and feedback, which can all bolster your mindset for success. A well-chosen mentor can function as a compass guiding you to your definition of success.

A significant aspect of mindset development also involves fostering self-compassion. Oftentimes, we are our own harshest critic, which can erode our self-confidence and halt our progress. Embracing self-compassion allows us to forgive ourselves for our mistakes, viewing them as opportunities for growth, rather than personal failures.

Mindfulness is another vital component for cultivating a successful mindset. By staying present, we can fully engage in our tasks and decisions, leading to more thoughtful and intentional actions. This, in turn, helps us to make more effective and productive choices that aligns with our goals.

Maintaining a positive outlook is key in developing a Growth Mindset. While it's natural to feel disappointed or frustrated when things go wrong, it's essential to see these instances as temporary setbacks rather than final outcomes. Optimism encourages resilience and keeps us focused on our long-term goals, despite short-term obstacles.

Finally, cultivating a successful mindset also entails practicing gratitude. By appreciating what we already have and acknowledging the progress we've made, we can foster contentment and a healthy perspective towards success. Gratitude can also serve to ground us during periods of uncertainty and boost our overall wellbeing, both of which serve to nurture a Growth Mindset.

Keep in mind, shifting from a Fixed to a Growth Mindset is not an overnight transformation. It is a lifelong journey requiring consistent effort and introspection. However, understanding the central role of mindset in achieving success is a fundamental first step. You have the power to cultivate the mindset you desire - make sure it's one that aligns with your aspirations for success.

Belief Systems and Their Influence on Outcome

In the quest to achieve success, it's crucial to understand the significant role of belief systems. Our beliefs play a pivotal role in shaping our behavior, perspectives, and ultimately, our outcomes. In essence, our belief systems act as internal maps, guiding us towards or away from our desired goals.

Belief systems comprise of ingrained assumptions about ourselves, others, and how the world functions. They're the mental compass that influences our reactions and decisions. For instance, if one holds a belief that success is just about luck, they might not put in the necessary effort to realize their goals. Conversely, a belief in one's abilities can lead to increased effort, persistence, and ultimately, success.

Beliefs don't emerge out of a vacuum. They're a product of multiple influences including our upbringing, environment, experiences, cultural traditions, and even biological predispositions. While some beliefs are beneficial, facilitating personal growth and success, others can limit our potentials, holding us back from achieving what we desire.

It's no wonder we often speak about 'limiting beliefs.' These negative, self-defeating thoughts keep us stuck in unproductive patterns and hinder us from achieving NeuroSuccess. They're like roadblocks, obstructing us from moving forward. Identifying and changing these limiting beliefs is a crucial step towards cultivating a success-oriented mindset.

The influence of belief systems could be likened to a self-fulfilling prophecy. If we believe we're good at something, we're likely to be more motivated, invest more effort, and perform better. Similarly, if we harbor doubts about our capabilities or assume failure, it can lead to a decrease in effort, inducing a performance dip matching our negative expectations.

Interestingly, our belief systems do not just influence our behavior but also our physiology. Research has shown that the belief in ability to perform can boost performance by increasing physical endurance and reducing perception of effort. This aligns with the brain's adaptive nature, its plasticity, which allows it to change and evolve based on our thought processes.

Nevertheless, it's worth noting that the process of altering ingrained belief systems isn't quick nor easy. It's somewhat like trying to change the course of a river. Yet, with persistent efforts, it is indeed possible to reshape our minds. Cognitive Behavioral techniques, mindfulness, visualization, affirmations and positive self-talk are some powerful strategies for this neural rewiring.

Moreover, fostering positive beliefs is more than just 'thinking positive.' It's about changing our internal dialogue in a way that propels us forward. Not by denying reality or blindly throwing positivity around, but by choosing a perspective that recognizes potential, catalyzes effort, and engenders resilience.

Think about the process of cultivating a success-oriented belief system as planting a garden. Discarding limiting beliefs is akin to weeding out unproductive plants, making room for the growth of beneficial ones. Continually nurturing the garden is the key to its flourishing, just as steadfastly fostering positive beliefs is crucial for NeuroSuccess.

Moreover, the strength of our belief systems hinges on consistency. Just like the repeating patterns of a song are what make it 'catchy,' repeating positive belief practices help strengthen those neural connections in our brains. The more often we engage in an activity or thought process, the more 'familiar' and 'natural' it becomes for our brain, facilitating smoother navigation towards our goals.

While altering belief systems, it's also essential to take into account your individual attributes. After all, every brain is unique, and so are our belief systems. Therefore, what might work for someone else in changing their beliefs may not necessarily work for you.

Belief systems and their influence on outcomes extend beyond personal achievement or success. They also impact our relationships, career progress, health, and overall well-being, hence reaffirming their enormous influence. Recognizing and understanding the power of belief systems offer the key to unlocking new potentials, nurturing growth, and achieving NeuroSuccess.

In conclusion, belief systems hold a tremendous influence over our outcomes. The thoughts we entertain, both consciously and subconsciously, shape our behavior, actions, and eventually our outcomes. Recognizing this power sets the stage for transformation, offering an insightful path to change our mindset and achieve success.

By understanding the core elements of our belief systems and consistently working towards altering them in favour of success-oriented beliefs, we can harness the potential of our brains to guide us towards our desired outcomes. This is the essence of NeuroSuccess - the deliberate retraining of our brain towards self-improvement and success.

Chapter 3: Barriers to NeuroSuccess

As we embark on this transformative journey to NeuroSuccess, it's vital to acknowledge and address the roadblocks that may hinder us. Our inner enemies – fear, doubt, and procrastination – can often inhibit our brain's ability to adapt and change, potentially derailing our pursuit of true success. Yet, these internal foes are not the sole perpetrators of stagnation. In our hyper-connected society, external distractions constantly compete for our brain's attention, detracting from our cognitive resources needed for personal and professional growth. Moreover, past failures and emotional trauma can forge neural pathways resistant to change out of a fundamental human instinct to avoid discomfort and pain. By recognizing and understanding these barriers, we're better equipped to collaboratively work with our brain — not against it — capitalizing on its plasticity and optimizing its performance.

The Enemies Within: Fear, Doubt, and Procrastination

We all have internal foes that hinder our progress towards our goals. The most prominent among these saboteurs are fear, doubt, and procrastination. They act as barriers to NeuroSuccess by hampering our potential to unleash the full power of our brain.

Fear is the instinctive response to potential harm or pain: it manifests as an insidious preventing factor when it comes to stepping out of our comfort zones. Engaging in anything unfamiliar or challenging breeds a certain level of fear, creating a mental barrier that keeps us inside our familiar boundaries. This, inevitably, stunts our growth. Let it be emphasized: fear isn't something to be completely eliminated or wrong in itself. It only becomes a negative factor when it paralyzes us from taking action and exploring new territories.

Doubt, the second enemy within, is usually experienced when we lack faith in our abilities or find our goals too ambitious to attain. Its effect can be devastating as it undermines our self-confidence, leading to immobilization and failure. The real danger of doubt is its intrinsic ability to hide itself away, only to surface when we're about to take a significant step forward. It fuels indecision and keeps us from reaching our true potential.

Procrastination, our third adversary, impedes our progress by pushing us to delay essential tasks. It's a manifestation of avoiding discomfort and favors instant gratification over long-term achievement. It's the brain's way of taking the easy road instead of the difficult one. One must remember, however, that procrastination is not merely a reflection of laziness—it's a complex psychological challenge that needs concrete strategies to overcome.

First and foremost, we must accept these internal enemies are part of being human. That's not to say we should let them control us, but understanding their presence can help us develop strategies to combat them effectively. We can't fight an invisible enemy, but once we recognize them, we can work to overcome their negative impact.

It's critical to remember that fear, doubt, and procrastination don't necessarily imply that we lack motivation or lack the will to succeed. These internal blocks can occur even when we're deeply committed to our goals. It's not a lack of desire, but the presence of internal conflict that holds us back.

Engaging fear begins with understanding it for what it is: a natural human response designed to protect us from harm. But in our modern world, much of what we fear doesn't pose any physical danger to us. Once we realize this fact, we can examine our fears and reframe them. Reframing fear involves turning it into a guide, an indicator that we're stepping into new territory, moving out of our comfort zones, and exploring our full potential.

Doubt requires a different approach. Cultivating self-confidence and improving self-worth are potent strategies to overcome it. Instead of giving into the discomfort that doubt breeds, redirect your thoughts into a more positive outlook. Encourage an internal dialogue that reinforces your abilities, achievements, and unique qualities. Empower yourself with the belief that any dream, despite its magnitude, can be achieved with determination, patience, and resilience.

When taking on procrastination, we must debunk the myth that it's merely a bad habit that can be broken by willpower alone. In reality, overcoming procrastination requires a better understanding of one's internal reward system and a series of actionable steps to create a conducive environment for productivity. The power of immediate gratification must be recognized, and the methodology to delay it must be learned.

To counteract these enemies within, exerting willpower and discipline won't always suffice. Instead, considerable work needs to be done on "reprogramming" these instincts. This is done by creating new neural pathways in the brain more aligned with success and positivity. It involves setting up new automatic responses that favor growth and achievement over fear, doubt, and delay.

These internal barriers are universal, and they can be formidable obstacles when mismanaged. But when rightly approached and consciously addressed, fears can be catalysts for growth, doubt can be transformed into motivation, and procrastination can be reshaped into strategic delay. It's a process that relies heavily on understanding, patience, and self-kindness.

In the following sections, we'll delve deeper into how procrastination disrupts the smooth workings of the brain and how it can stealthily kill dreams. A detailed exploration of strategies to overcome this delay and avoidance will follow. Also, we will discuss the transformation from procrastination to action through a considerable neural shift.

Furthermore, we will explore brain-training techniques and strategies designed to help you harness the full potential of your brain for wealth and achievement. We will discuss the power of visualization, mindfulness, and positive self-talk, and how these can help reprogram your neural wiring for success.

Remember, overcoming these internal enemies and achieving NeuroSuccess is not a quick fix—it demands dedication, patience, and consistent action. It's a journey of growth, transformation, and personal discovery in which the destination is a life driven by a powerhouse of a brain that embraces success as its natural state.

We all have the capacity to achieve NeuroSuccess; all it takes is recognizing and combatting our inner enemies, understanding our brain's workings, and reprogramming it for success. A fascinating journey awaits you, filled with challenges, surprises, and sure victories on your path to NeuroSuccess. Let's embrace the journey and move towards our desired destinations.

External Distractions and Their Cognitive Impact

Now that we've talked about the internal barriers to success, let's turn our attention to the external ones. Focusing particularly on distractions, which can be disruptive in our journey to achieve NeuroSuccess. The world is full of potential distractions - from our devices constantly begging for our attention to noisy environments that disrupt our concentration.

Firstly, to understand the cognitive impact of these external distractions, we need to delve into what happens in the brain when it encounters a distraction. One of the key brain structures affected by distractions is the prefrontal cortex. This forward part of the brain orchestrates high-level cognitive processes such as focusing our attention, planning, and decision making.

When we're exposed to an external distraction, it fights for our attention. If it prevails, it suddenly starts commanding the prefrontal cortex's attention, causing it to abort its current cognitive task. This distraction triggers a neural pathway that leads to disruptive shifts in focus. Consequently, you find it harder to resume the initial cognitive task, and your cognitive processing becomes slower and less efficient.

Moreover, excessive external distractions can lead to cognitive overload, a state where the brain's processing capacity is challenged by too much information at once. This can result in decreased memory performance and impaired cognitive abilities. In other words, frequent and intense distractions compromise our overall mental performance and productivity.

Quite notably, the digital interruptions that technology brings have a significant cognitive impact. Modern society bombards us with a rapid-fire stream of notifications, updates, and alerts. Each time our phone buzzes, or a pop-up appears on our computer, our focus instantly shifts from our ongoing task to that digital interruption. It's a consistent disruption that makes piercing focus on a single task increasingly difficult.

Research has shown that these digital distractions, such as checking your email or a rush to respond to a text message, can reduce your effective IQ by an average of 10 points. This drop is even higher than the cognitive impact of smoking marijuana or losing a night's sleep. It's clear that these short, frequent interruptions have a measurable cognitive impact.

Uncontrolled exposure to external distractions can also induce chronic stress, leading to the release of stress hormones such as cortisol. This is damaging for the brain and can inhibit the growth and branching of neurons, particularly affecting areas like the hippocampus that plays a critical role in memory and learning. So, in the long run, being persistently distracted could negatively impact brain health and cognitive function.

Apart from digital distractions, let's not forget environmental distractions like noise pollution, visual clutter, or people intruding on your space. A noisy environment can escalate cognitive load, causing heightened stress and impaired productivity. Likewise, visual clutter in your work or home environment can compete for your attention, resulting in inefficient focus and diminished cognitive performance.

Physical interruptions by colleagues or family members can be another source of distraction. While human interaction is certainly necessary and beneficial, it can also be disruptive when it happens too frequently or at an inopportune moment.

It may seem like we're powerless in the face of these distractions, but in reality, we have more control than we think. Understanding how distractions interfere with your brain's functioning is the first step toward mitigating their impact.

By creating focused strategies to limit the influence of these distractions, we can misdirect our attention and reduce the cognitive cost of switching between tasks. This will subsequently improve our productivity, boost our performance, and help us keep track of our true path to success.

We'll explore these strategies in more detail in future chapters, honing in on the methods to declutter our digital and physical spaces, incorporating beneficial habits, and setting boundaries with the people around us.

In the end, developing the brain's ability to remain focused despite distractions is a critical component of NeuroSuccess. Understanding the cognitive impact of these distractions provides a vital rationale for taking deliberate steps towards cultivating a richer, more focused internal environment.

Overcoming Past Failures and Emotional Trauma

Moving forward from the last section, we're going to explore a crucial barrier to achieving NeuroSuccess. Trauma and past failures can form stubborn roadblocks on the path to success, hindering progress, and fostering negative self-perceptions. Learning how to navigate these life events, accepting them, and transforming them into valuable life lessons are significant steps toward enabling our brains for success.

First, we need to demystify the concept of failure and the negative connotations we often attach to it. Failures are not the end; they're simply moments of learning, providing lessons that couldn't have been taught otherwise. The inventor Thomas Edison, who famously failed 10,000 times before creating a viable light bulb, once said, "I haven't failed. I've just found 10,000 ways that won't work." Hence, there is a need to redefine failure in our minds as a stepping stone towards success.

Next, let's address how to overcome the shadow of past failures. One technique is to practice mindfulness, which essentially means staying in the present moment. It's easy to get stuck on past mistakes, but it's vital to realize that these past events have already happened and can't be changed. Instead, focus on what you can do in the present moment, applying the lessons of past failures. Acceptance of this concept is a powerful way to move forward.

Another vital strategy is to let go of your fear of repeating past failures. This fear can be paralyzing, but it's often irrational. Understand that growth involves taking risks and occasionally failing. Instead of fearing past failures, use them to strategize for future success.

Emotional trauma, too, can create significant barriers to growth and success. This can range from childhood adversity to a significant emotional event in adulthood. Emotional trauma isn't easy to confront, and it's okay to seek professional help if you need it. Engaging with a trained therapist or psychiatrist can provide you with coping mechanisms and strategies to heal and move forward.

Apart from seeking professional help, developing a strong emotional support system plays a significant role in dealing with trauma. Sharing your experiences, pain, and healing journey can be cathartic and help ease the burden of trauma. Make sure you surround yourself with people who understand, respect, and support your journey.

Furthermore, engaging in self-care practices can greatly help in overcoming emotional trauma. This includes maintaining a healthy lifestyle, getting enough sleep, eating a balanced diet, and regular physical activity. Practices such as meditation and mindfulness can allow for self-reflection and introspection, enabling you to understand and process your emotions better.

Journaling is also a beneficial method of dealing with trauma and past failures. Writing about your experiences can provide a medium to express and organize your thoughts and emotions. It also helps in deskilling negative cognitive patterns and gradually replacing them with positive thoughts, leading to improved mood and emotional well-being.

Lastly, adopting the practice of gratitude can significantly help overcome past failures and emotional trauma. Gratitude shifts the focus from your past failures and hardships to the positive aspects and accomplishments of your life. It encourages a positive outlook, which is imperative for long-term success and happiness.

It's important to remember that healing from trauma and overcoming past failures is a process. It takes time. Impatience and the desire for a quick fix only lead to frustration and setback. Patience and perseverance are key elements in this journey to NeuroSuccess.

Cultivating resilience is critical on this path. Willingly facing your past failures and emotional traumas, and using them as catalysts for growth, is what defines resilience. It involves an intrinsic motivation to strive for better, despite the hurdles encountered.

Undeniably, overcoming past failures and emotional trauma can be challenging and intimidating. But remember, the biggest growth often occurs when we step out of our comfort zones. See these challenges not as insurmountable obstacles but opportunities for learning and personal growth.

In a nutshell, confronting our past failures and emotional trauma, redefining our perception of failure, and developing resilience are fundamental steps towards achieving NeuroSuccess. It is not a smooth path, but the journey and its enlightening experiences make it worthwhile.

After comprehending and implementing these strategies, you'll be well-equipped to recognize and assess the barriers you may have to NeuroSuccess. Moving forward, the next chapter dives into one of the most prevalent and silent dream killers—procrastination, a hindrance that keeps us from realizing our full potential. There, we'll delve into the neuroscience behind procrastination and offer strategies to shift from delay to action.

Chapter 4: Procrastination: The Silent Dream Killer

Understanding and overcoming procrastination is one of the most vital steps towards NeuroSuccess. Procrastination, often disguised as a benign habit, is a silent killer of dreams, and it's integral to comprehend the neuroscience behind it. Derived from the network of neurons in our brain, procrastination is a battle between the prefrontal cortex, the detailed planner, and the limbic system, a pleasure-seeking immediate gratifier. While the terms might seem daunting, in simple terms, it's your mind's struggle between what you should be doing and what you want to do. Overcoming this hurdle requires us to put certain strategies into play that propel us from avoidance to action. Bridging this gap requires rewiring your brain's pathways, and with persistence, you can make this shift. The most empowering facet of brain plasticity is that although procrastination might seem to have made itself at home in your daily routine, it's temporary and changeable.

The Neuroscience Behind Procrastination

Procrastination is not merely a bad habit or a moral failing - it's a complex psychological challenge that involves the brain in ways you may not have considered. In exploring the neuroscience behind procrastination, we delve into the components of the brain that are most involved in this self-defeating behavior.

The brain's prefrontal cortex, where executive function takes place, is largely responsible for planning tasks and making decisions. It's the more rational, sensible part of the brain that pushes you to do your work or complete a task. This area is especially impacted when we procrastinate, it's not fully developed in humans until their mid-20s and is easily overwhelmed by distractions and short-term gratification.

On the other hand, the limbic system, one of the most dominant portions of the brain, is involved with emotions and drives, and it seeks immediate satisfaction. If the limbic system is more compelling at any given moment, you'll likely give in to what it wants—hence, procrastination.

The amygdala, another critical part of the limbic system, is known for its role in fear processing. An overactive amygdala can stimulate fear or anxiety. When faced with a daunting task, the amygdala may generate a fear reaction, causing you to avoid the task and seek comfort in less challenging or more enjoyable activities—a perfect recipe for procrastination.

Research suggests that the stress hormone cortisol plays a significant part too. It's released in response to perceived stressful situations, activating the amygdala and suppressing the prefrontal cortex. High cortisol levels can thus promote fear-induced procrastination.

Another piece of the puzzle is dopamine, the neurotransmitter linked to the reward system in the brain. Dopamine reinforces the rewarding feeling you get when you give in to procrastination, such as engaging in leisure activities instead of pressing tasks.

Understanding this, you begin to see that procrastination isn't just about willpower or time management. It's a clash between different brain systems, each with its agenda, influenced by a cocktail of chemical neurotransmitters.

So, is there a biological predisposition to procrastinate? Studies suggest that yes, procrastination has genetic roots. Certain genes influencing dopamine regulation are linked to a tendency to procrastinate, indicating a biological vulnerability for this behavior.

Neuroimaging studies offer more insights into the procrastinating brain. Some research shows that individuals who tend to procrastinate have a larger amygdala and a weaker connection between this structure and the dorsal part of the anterior cingulate cortex (dorsal ACC). The dorsal ACC uses information from the amygdala to decide whether to carry on with a task or abandon it. In procrastinators, this link is weaker, making it tougher for them to press on with tasks that might lead to negative outcomes.

While these insights paint a picture of inherent biological challenges, they shouldn't be viewed as immutable. Remember, the brain is plastic; its structure and function can be modified with experience and training. Officers, coaches, teachers, and other people can alter the procrastination patterns in their brains by reshaping these neural pathways.

One technique found to help is mindfulness—the nonjudgmental focus on the present moment. Regular practice of mindfulness can strengthen the prefrontal cortex and reduce the reactivity of the amygdala, thereby promoting more adaptive responses to stress and challenges instead of procrastination.

Physical exercise is another potent tool to improve your brain health and fight procrastination. Exercise enhances your overall brain function, including the areas linked to self-control and executive function. It also reduces cortisol and boosts mood-enhancing chemicals like serotonin and dopamine, which can help offset the quick fix of immediate gratification.

Before moving on to specific strategies to overcome procrastination in the next section, remember this: you're not just fighting a "bad habit." You're dealing with different parts of your brain battling each other for dominance. But with an understanding of the neuroscience at play and the right strategies and practices, you can tilt the battle in favor of productivity and effectiveness.

Given these insights into the neuroscience of procrastination, it's crucial not to beat yourself up over this behavior. Instead, view it as a part of your brain's make-up, a well-intentioned but misguided attempt to avoid discomfort or fear. The key to overcoming procrastination isn't to scold or berate yourself, but to understand and gently redirect your brain behavior.

As we prepare to explore concrete strategies to overcome procrastination, remember: you are already taking a crucial step forward in understanding the neuroscience behind it. And with knowledge comes the power to change.

Strategies to Overcome Delay and Avoidance

Now that we've explored procrastination in depth, we need to formulate strategies to conquer it. Attack it head-on, by first identifying your procrastination patterns. Are there specific tasks or situations that trigger your avoidance? Recognizing these patterns is a critical first step to overcoming procrastination.

Once you've identified your patterns, the next strategy is to practice self-compassion. Don't beat yourself up over procrastination. Self-critical thoughts only create more barriers for you. Instead, acknowledge that you're human, and like any other human, you aren't immune to the temptation of avoidance.

Next, it's crucial to break tasks into manageable sub-tasks. This simple strategy goes a long way because big, ambiguous tasks are intimidating, which often feed procrastination. When you break down a large task, it decreases the cognitive load and makes the task seem achievable, thereby reducing the tendency to procrastinate.

Using the power of visualization also aids in overcoming delays. Instead of visualizing the apparent chaos of a hard, tedious task, envision the satisfaction you'll feel once the task is done. Visualizing positive outcomes and emotions helps to motivate you into taking action.

Additionally, the Pomodoro Technique is worth mentioning. Here, you break your work into twenty-five-minute intervals, each followed by a short break. This time management technique helps keep your focus sharp and reduce your propensity for procrastination by sustaining momentum and rewarding progress.

Tackling your most important and challenging tasks first thing in the morning is another beneficial strategy. This is often referred to as 'eating the frog.' Most people have a higher capacity for focused work early in the day. By completing your most demanding task first, you set a productive tone for the rest of your day.

Creating a prioritized to-do list is a method that's been proven effective to help overcome delay and avoidance too. By identifying and organizing what needs to be done and in what order, you structure your tasks in a way that maximizes efficiency and minimizes procrastination.

Furthermore, setting clear, achievable goals is also necessary to steer clear of procrastination. The clearer and more specific the goals, the easier it is to take immediate action. If your goals are too vague or too ambitious, it's more likely you'll succumb to procrastination.

Next on the list is using effective tools, both digital and traditional, to aid in organization. Calendar apps, project management tools, or a simple notebook can all serve the purpose of helping manage tasks and deadlines.

Building healthy habits is another strategy that's part of our fight against procrastination. When you spend time nurturing good habits, you'll naturally have less time to delay or avoid essential tasks.

Moreover, blocking distractions is a practical approach to staying focused on tasks. Isolating yourself from physical disruptions, turning off notifications on your devices, or even using apps that limit your time on certain distracting websites can significantly improve your productivity.

While willpower is a considerable factor in overcoming procrastination, it's strengthened by maintaining good health. Regular physical exercise, a balanced diet, and adequate sleep can boost your energy, focus, and overall cognitive power. With improved cognitive functioning, you're better equipped to tackle procrastination head-on.

Lastly, understand that overcoming procrastination is not about perfection; it's about progress. You're bound to have days when you'll procrastinate. On such occasions, remind yourself of your larger objective, pull yourself together, and continue pushing forward.

These strategies and others covered in the book can empower you to break the habit of procrastination and replace it with productivity. But remember, overcoming delay and avoidance doesn't happen overnight; it's a process that involves consistency and patience. Arm yourself with these strategies, and you're well on your way to winning the battle against procrastination.

From Procrastination to Action: A Neural Shift

The road to success is often blocked by one major roadblock: procrastination. However, this does not have to be the end of the story. By understanding the neural mechanisms behind procrastination, you can begin to take steps towards making a positive shift - from delay to action.

Procrastination, for a long time, has been viewed as a symptom of laziness or lack of discipline. However, neuroscience offers a different perspective. Procrastination can be traced back to the brain's natural response to perceived stressors or threats. It's a protective mechanism, dictated by our primal instincts, which includes feelings of fear, discomfort, or just the plain uncertainty of success.

So, how do we make a shift from delaying tasks to taking decisive action? The essential first step is learning how to change your brain's response to these perceived threats. Moving from a reactive to proactive state of mind requires a deliberate choice to regularly engage our prefrontal cortex - the rational, problem-solving part of our brain. By doing so, we can override our instinctive responses and establish a new, positive neural pathway.

One strategy that can help is practicing mindfulness. Mindfulness involves being fully present and engaged in the current task, rather than getting lost in a whirlwind of thoughts and worries about the future. This helps to alleviate the stress or fear that may trigger procrastination, allowing you to focus on the task at hand.

Another tool to consider is mental visualization. By envisioning yourself successfully completing a task before you begin, you can prime your brain for success. This not only boosts your confidence but reduces the perceived threats that activate procrastination. Visualization encourages your brain to focus on potential rewards rather than risks, promoting action over delay.

In addition to mindfulness and visualization, it's important to balance your brain's reward system. Our brains tend to procrastinate when they predict more punishment than reward from a task. Thus, introducing small rewards when you finish tasks can stimulate your brain's reward centers, prompting you to take action more often.

Remember, tackling procrastination is not about mustering the willpower to force yourself to work. It's more about training your brain to recognize that the perceived threats prompting procrastination are not as daunting as they seem. By rewiring your neural responses to these situations, you can gradually shift from a state of constant delay and deferral to proactive action-taking.

Naturally, this neural shift won't occur overnight. It's a process that involves patience, practice, and persistence. Each time that you override the urge to procrastinate and take action instead, you reinforce this new neural pathway. Over time, this pathway becomes stronger and more automatic, thereby transforming the once arduous task of initiation into a natural response.

Undeniably, we also have to adjust our environments to support this neural shift. Reducing external distractions, setting specific goals, and breaking tasks down into manageable portions can further ease the transition from procrastination to action. The key is to make the process of getting started more inviting and less overwhelming.

While the phrase "Mind over Matter" might seem cliché, it resonates strongly with our discussion here. Making a neural shift from procrastination to action requires a blend of understanding your brain and applying strategies that promote action over delay. It brings to light the immense power that lies in our neural networks and the possibility to harness this power to overcome self-imposed barriers like procrastination.

Furthermore, realize that everyone procrastinates sometimes. It's universal, and it's human. Instead of self-criticism, you should focus on understanding your brain and training it to respond differently. Also, remember that success isn't the absence of procrastination but the ability to move past it.

In conclusion, the journey from procrastination to action requires a deliberate and sustained brain retraining process. Once you establish the new neural pathways that influence instant action, you'll find yourself stepping into a world of greater productivity, efficiency, and ultimately, success. The power to shift from procrastination to action, indeed, lies within the extraordinary plasticity of our brains. Embrace it, and change the course of your journey towards success.

By adopting these methods and understanding the neurology behind procrastination, one can retrain their brain from habits of procrastination to habits of action, driving towards a more goal-oriented life and successful future.

Chapter 5: Brain-Training Techniques for Wealth and Achievement

Having examined the pivotal role procrastination plays in sapping our potential of achieving success, we now venture into transformative techniques that will help retrain our brain for wealth-creation and accomplishment. While vision drives action, it's the power of visualization - vividly picturing objectives, results, and the route to success – that serves as an invigorating ignition for your brain's success engine. There's also the indispensability of mindfulness and meditation for clear thinking, which help declutter the mind and enhance focus on what's essential. The neural rewiring can be further reinforced through affirmations and positive self-talk; these create a soothing melodic rhythm that drowns the nagging noise of self-doubt and negativity. Finally, we delve into cognitive-behavior strategies for success. These potent techniques will help shape cognitions and behaviors into the best version of one's self, on a relentless pursuit of success. As we traverse each technique, let's assimilate and apply the knowledge concurrently, strengthening our neural pathways to wealth and achievement with each newfound insight.

The Power of Visualization

Having discussed the foundations of success and brain-training techniques, it's necessary to delve into a key tool in achieving your goals. Welcome to the world of visualization. It isn't just an abstract concept; it's a potent cognitive tool sparking your brain to work towards your set goals to manifest them into reality. This technique leverages the power of our mind's eye to propel us towards our envisioned dreams.

Visualization is a form of mental rehearsal where you imagine and experience your desired outcomes within your mind. The process involves creating images, sensations, or emotions relating to a particular event or objective you wish to manifest. When we vividly imagine our dreams and goals—be it securing that promotion or publishing that book—we are essentially 'practicing' in a simulation created by our brain. This seemingly simple act can have a profound impact on our path to success.

Now, it's crucial to understand the neuroscience that grounds the power of visualization. Our brain has a network of neurons, which are its operational unit. These neurons communicate through a process of firing electrical signals and releasing chemicals, allowing us to think, imagine, and perform actions. When we visualize, we are 'activating' these neurons, training ourselves for the goal we desire. This process, known as synaptic plasticity, propels cognitive restructuring, which can influence our thoughts, behaviors, and attitudes favorably toward achieving our ambitions.

But how does visualization help in achieving success? A fundamental principle underpinning visualization is the 'Mind-Body Connection'. Our brain can't distinguish between a vivid imagination and the actual occurrence of an event. It will respond to visualized images as though they are happening in reality, releasing corresponding hormones and signals. For instance, if you visualize yourself giving a successful presentation, your brain interprets it as a real event, increasing your confidence and reducing anxiety.

Visualization aids in motivation. By regularly envisioning your goals and the associated benefits, you're continually reminding yourself of what you're aiming for. This can be incredibly motivating and can provide you the impetus you need to push through challenges and overcome obstacles. A picture of your end goal can be an exceptionally compelling motivation booster, keeping you focused and inspired along your journey.

Moreover, visualization utilizes the 'Law of Attraction'—a popular psychological concept which postulates that 'positive thoughts lead to positive outcomes'. This doesn't imply that merely imagining success will make it manifest magically. Rather, it suggests that consistently positive mental rehearsals increase positive self-perception and optimism, leading to increased determination, resilience, and productive actions—critical components for driving success.

The practice of visualization doesn't have to be a time-consuming endeavor. Regularity and consistency are more important than length. Set aside a few moments each day, find a calm and quiet surrounding, sit comfortably, and start with deep, mindful breathing. Then imagine your desired outcome in detail, including not just visual images but also associate emotions, smells, touch, and sound to create a near-real scenario. Experience the sense of achievement, fulfillment, and delight tied to achieving your goal.

This technique isn't just a modern-day buzzword but is rooted in ancient times. From athletes using it to enhance their performance to businessmen applying it to improve their venture's success, the application of visualization is diverse and well-documented over history.

However, like any other brain-training technique, visualization isn't a one-size-fits-all solution to success. It's a tool that works best when combined with realistic goal setting, strategic planning, and consistent hard work. Visualization isn't a shortcut to success; it's a tool to bolster your psychological arsenal to accomplish your aspirations more efficiently and effectively.

There is a caveat, though. Visualization involves a subtle balance. While it's essential to imagine positive outcomes, it can't spiral into daydreaming or lead to unrealistic expectations. As powerful as visualization is, it shouldn't be used to create an unrealistic, perfect world where things always go according to plan. Life will invariably present obstacles and challenges, no matter how extensively you visualize. Therefore, maintaining a grounded approach is necessary for turning your visualized ambitions into tangible reality.

Embrace the power of visualization to train your brain towards your goals. It may seem daunting initially, but remember, like any skill, it just takes a little practice. With perseverance and consistency, you'll soon find this powerful tool ingrained into your journey of success.

To conclude, harness the power of visualization to induce a shift in your mindset and attitude, helping your brain adapt to new possibilities. Visualization is an effective tool, a stepping stone that can aid you in climbing the ladder of success. However, remember, it must be employed judiciously alongside other brain-training techniques and pro-active actions. Achieve your milestones and pave the way towards realizing your dreams.

Mindfulness and Meditation for Clear Thinking

Meditation and mindfulness are terms that have gained popularity in recent years, but their benefits to mental clarity are age-old. Mindfulness, the practice of being present and fully engaged with whatever we're doing at the moment — free from distraction or judgment, and aware of our thoughts and feelings without getting caught up in them — can change the way we work.

Meditation, which can be viewed as a deep state of concentration, allows us to focus our attention, eliminating the stream of jumbled thoughts that crowd our minds and cause stress. Many forms of meditation exist, but most involve a quiet environment, comfortable posture, focused attention, and an open attitude. Regular practice enhances mental clarity, creativity, and cognitive flexibility.

So, how do meditation and mindfulness connect to promoting clear thinking and propelling us towards success? We first need to understand that our minds are complex mechanisms. They have a tendency to wander off, reminiscing about the past or focusing on the future.

By practicing mindfulness, we train our minds to stay in the present. Engaging in this way allows us to focus on tasks more effectively, improving our job performance and productivity, and laying the groundwork for achieving our goals. Mindfulness promotes a non-judgmental awareness of our thoughts, providing us with more perspective and choice in how we respond to life's situations.

Incorporating mindfulness into our daily routine doesn't have to be an overtly spiritual or time-consuming endeavor; it can as simple as engaging all your senses while eating or really listening when someone is speaking to you. It's about fully immersing yourself in the task at hand, whether it's writing a report or washing the dishes.

Meditation, on the other hand, offers its own clear-thinking benefits. By training our minds to focus without distraction, we enhance our cognitive control. Cognitive control refers to the abilities that allow us to direct our attention and think abstractly. This not only makes us more effective at conducing mentally challenging tasks, but also equips us to better manage stress and self-regulate our emotions.

A regular meditation practice can be incorporated in a variety of ways, from dedicated meditation sessions to mini meditation breaks throughout the day. A practice as short as five minutes every morning can have a significant impact on your cognitive control and ability to focus. All you need is a quiet space and willingness to direct your attention to your breath, a mantra, or even the feeling of sitting.

In a fast-paced world where distraction reigns, the focus and mental clarity facilitated by mindfulness and meditation practices are invaluable assets. The ability to stay present, to focus intently, and to think clearly significantly improves decision-making abilities and problem-solving skills — driving forces of success.

Not only does mindfulness and meditation improve clarity and focus, they can also foster emotional well-being. By observing our thoughts and emotions from a neutral perspective, we can learn to unravel negative thought patterns and create new, more positive ones. This emotional balancing act can foster resilience, reduce stress and anxiety, and promote a sense of peace and calm.

Moreover, mindfulness and meditation can have strong physiological effects, including decreased blood pressure and heart rate, improved sleep quality, and even beneficial changes in areas of the brain associated with memory, sense of self, and empathy. "Mindfulness and meditation are exercises for the brain. Just as physical exercise strengthens the body, these mental exercises can help keep our brain agile and healthy," says

While both mindfulness and meditation support clear thinking, they are not one-size-fits-all solutions. Each individual's experience with these practices will be unique. Some people may find more clarity through silent meditation, while others might prefer mindful yoga or walking. The key is to explore and find what resonates with you.

The practice of mindfulness and meditation helps in grounding ourselves and reduces fluctuations of the mind. As a result, we experience improved awareness, cognition, emotional intelligence, and health-related quality of life. Clear thinking, in turn, leads to more effective problem solving, better decision making, and increased creativity, which are essential components of success.

So, in conclusion, adding mindfulness and meditation into our life is like adding another tool to our success toolkit. They may feel unfamiliar or even strange at first, but like any skill, they improve with practice.

Start small, experiment to find practices that work for you and, most importantly, be patient with yourself during the process. Remember, success is not a sprint; it's a marathon. And cultivating mindfulness and meditation habits for clear thinking can be the stepping stones to paving your path to achieving success.

Affirmations and Positive Self-talk: The Neural Rewiring

With the foundations of success, the power of visualization, and the calming influence of mindfulness and meditation under our belt, it's time to delve into another powerful technique for brain training. This is the power of affirmations and positive self-talk - a tool directly aimed at neural rewiring.

The human brain is a natural pattern-seeker, constantly scanning our interactions and experiences for meaning. When these patterns consist of negative thinking and self-talk, the brain becomes primed for this negativity and is shaped around these thoughts. However, the power of affirmations and positive self-talk can rewire this circuitry, effectively reprogramming the brain with uplifting and constructive messages.

Before we jump into the utilization of affirmations and positive self-talk, it's vital to understand the underlying science. The principle working behind these techniques is neuroplasticity, which refers to the brain's natural ability to form new neural connections throughout life. This is the key to 'rewiring' the brain for positive change.

Affirmations are positive, specific statements that help you to overcome self-sabotaging, negative thoughts. They help you visualize and believe in what you're affirming to yourself, creating the image in your brain of achieving what you want. As you verbalize these positive messages, you're effectively teaching your brain to believe these messages over time.

As for positive self-talk, it involves speaking to yourself, either out loud or in your mind, in a supportive, understanding, and motivational manner. By speaking to yourself in the way you would speak to a dear friend, you bring about a positive internal dialogue that strengthens self-esteem and promotes a healthier view of oneself and one's abilities.

Building affirmations and conducting positive self-talk is like carving a path through a dense forest. Each day, as you repeat your positive statements, you're forging a trail, making it easier to travel each time. With sustained practice, the brain starts to strengthen these newly formed neural pathways, making the positive messages a part of your subconscious, a set-in-stone way of thinking and behaving.

The key to effective affirmations is to ensure they are present tense, positive, personal, and precise. For instance, instead of saying "I will become successful," you might say, "I am becoming more successful every day." This approach makes the statement immediate and potent, and your brain perceives it as reality.

Implementing positive self-talk begins with recognizing and intercepting negative self-talk. When you recognize you're speaking harshly to yourself, take a pause, and rephrase the message in a compassionate and realistic way. For example, instead of saying "I'm terrible at this," you might say, "I'm still learning and improving."

Strategically incorporating affirmations and positive self-talk in your daily routine can help initiate this neural rewiring process. Here are a few practical ways to do so. Start your day with a positive affirmation and let it be the first and last thought of your day. Maintain an affirmation journal, recording your affirmations, self-talk, and perceptions noticed throughout the day. Use a mirror to perform positive self-talk. Looking into your own eyes while affirming positive messages can immensely intensify the experience.

It's vital to practice affirmations and positive self-talk regularly for the best results. Consistency is key here. You're not likely to believe a positive message about yourself the first time you say it. However, over time your brain will begin to accept that these positive thoughts are the truth about you and your abilities.

Remember, it's okay if some days are tougher than others. Don't be hard on yourself if positivity seems challenging to summon consistently. Progress can be slow and gradual, and that's alright. The journey towards neural rewiring is a marathon, and each incremental step counts.

Merely rewriting your narrative, changing your internal dialogue, and repeating positive affirmations won't lead to an immediate shift in one's life. It's not a magic potion after all. Think of it as a piece of a jigsaw puzzle of change. Coupling this with other cognitive strategies, like visualization and mindfulness, and applying them to your goals and aspirations, constructs the recipe for effective neural rewiring, optimal brain health, and hence, success.

To conclude, positive self-talk and affirmations have the power to reshape our brain, our thinking patterns, and our perception of ourselves and our capabilities. They are powerful techniques that, with repeated and consistent practice, can gradually rewire our neural pathways. In the grand scheme, they steer us towards developing a healthier, positive mindset, overcoming barriers, and hence, unlocking success.

As we continue through this journey, we'll explore Cognitive Behavioral Strategies for Success in our next chapter, which use a problem-oriented method to address dysfunctions and distortions and their influence on one's actions and thoughts. Affirmations and positive self-talk can actually serve as an ideal complement to this approach, paving the way for increased self-awareness and improvement in one's thought process.

Cognitive Behavioral Strategies for Success

The term cognitive behavioral therapy (CBT) has origin roots in the psychological therapy realm. However, it is also a potent tool in the road to personal development and success. CBT hinges on the premise that our thoughts profoundly impact our emotions, leading to behavioral outcomes. With this therapy, we can rewire the mental processes and consequent actions that might hamper our progress towards success.

If the concept of CBT seems intimidating, or you think it's complicated, you're not alone. Nevertheless, it's a simple concept. Let's break it down: thoughts (cognition) affect feelings, and feelings impact behavior. It's that simple. So, if we can correctly manage and control our thoughts, we can influence our feelings and, by extension, our actions and outcomes. That's cognitive-behavioral therapy boiled down to its basics.

The first step in applying CBT for success is recognizing the thought patterns or beliefs ("cognitions") that are hindering your progress. These roadblocks might be self-doubts, fear of failure, or negative self-talk. It's vital to be brutally honest with yourself in this stage – it's the only way to truly bring these issues to light.

Once you identify these thought patterns, the next stage is to challenge them. Rationalize with them. Are these fears well-founded? Is the thought of failure omnipresent because of some past mishap? Maybe it's due to a fear that's been ingrained in you since childhood? Challenging these thoughts helps identify their origin, a critical part of the CBT process.

Once these detrimental thoughts are adequately identified and challenged, it's time to replace them. Swap out the negative thoughts with positive ones. Replace, "I can't succeed because I always fail" with "Every failure brings me one step closer to success". Replace, "I'm not as smart as others" with "We're all unique and have our strengths". You'd be amazed at how an optimistic twist to your thinking can alter your entire outlook and improve your chances at success.

Sometimes, implementing new thought patterns can seem daunting. You might encounter resistance to changing beliefs you've held for years. A helpful CBT technique to ease the transition is to start small. First, attack the less ingrained beliefs. For example, if you're often late and believe that it's impossible to be punctual, start there. Replacing the thought, "I'm never on time" with "I can be punctual by planning better" is a small, manageable step. Noticing the results of your punctuality will reinforce your new cognition and give you confidence to tackle bigger thought patterns next.

The CBT technique isn't an overnight process. It requires patience, persistence, and unyielding commitment. Reiterating your new beliefs needs to become your daily ritual. The more you converse with yourself, the more your new cogitations will become ingrained within you. And that's when you'll see shifts in your behavior, your mentality, and, eventually, your outcomes.

As you practice CBT, remember the essence of self-compassion. This journey isn't about being perfect—it's about progress. There'll be days when old thought patterns sneak their way back in. Instead of feeling defeated, remember that each day offers a new opportunity to reinforce positivity. Remind yourself that you're committed to change, acknowledge the setback, and press forward.

CBT can yield even greater benefits when paired with other needful practices. For instance, combining CBT with visualization exercises can significantly impact your success. While CBT helps reprogram negative thoughts, visualization reinforces your new, positive thoughts. You're reaffirming your refashioned beliefs by imagining your success, which further solidifies them in your subconscious.

It's crucial to maintain a journal of your CBT journey. Note the thoughts you're altering, how you're replacing them, and the effects observed. Tracking your progress allows for periodic reviews, adaptations where necessary and serves as a motivation when you start to see results. To this end, mindfulness and introspection are invaluable.

While it may initially seem uncomfortable or challenging, CBT is an incredibly powerful tool for reprogramming your thoughts and repositioning yourself for success. It's an acquired art—the more you practice, the better you'll become. So grab that journal, take that pause, and embark on this transformative journey. Remember, change starts from within, and your thought processes are the steering wheel to your success journey. Let CBT be your guide to the destination you desire, deserve, and genuinely can achieve.

Chapter 6: Building Habits for Long-Term Success

As we've explored in previous chapters, the brain's malleability is a potent tool in your quest for success. Still, without consistency and the formation of healthy routines, these gains can be transient. The truth is, well-crafted habits act like a bedrock for long-term achievement. Applying the science of habit formation is necessary for you to understand how neural connections are fortified and how routines become automated. It's not enough to initiate change—we need to sustain it. You'll need a concise arsenal of strategies for both building beneficial habits and breaking down those that set you back. The science of usurping negative patterns for positive ones can be a game-changer in your NeuroSuccess journey. Remember, though, that the power of these strategies lies, not in their conceptual understanding, but in their consistent application. It's like building a neuron castle—one brick at a time. Repeated actions, no matter how small, lead to exponential growth. They sequentially trigger neuronal changes and rewire the brain progressively, which is why consistency holds the key to neural reprogramming. Staying consistent bolsters the impacts of neural plasticity, solidifying habituated patterns that can become your scaffold for success.

The Science of Habit Formation

Transitioning from the realm of procrastination and delay to one of action and initiative, we delve deep into a territory that is pivotal to sustained success—habit formation. Habits can be thought of as the brain's way of building a code to perform specific tasks without the need of conscious decision-making or thought. This efficient mechanism of the brain allows us to carry out routine actions such as brushing our teeth or driving to work, use minimal cognitive effort.

To understand the science behind habit formation, it's crucial to recognize the 'Habit Loop.' This loop consists of three stages: the cue, the routine, and the reward. The cue is an event or trigger in your external or internal environment that kickstarts the habit process. The routine is the behavior you usually engage in reaction to the cue, and the reward is what you get from performing the routine—a positive outcome that reinforces the behavior.

The establishment of this loop and the forming of a habit banks significantly on the brain's efficiency. The role of habit formation is to conserve cognitive energy for more complex tasks, which requires the brain to automate some regular activities. It's for this reason that habits, once formed, are challenging to break.

One of the critical sites within the brain related to habit formation is the basal ganglia, a structure tucked deep inside the cerebral hemispheres. The basal ganglia are crucial for the formation and maintenance of habits, as well as other functions such as motor control and learning.

When you start performing a new task, the pre-frontal cortex, the brain's decision-making center, works in overdrive. Because this area requires relatively high energy levels to function, it tries to pass off familiar tasks to the basal ganglia, which handles these tasks with impressive efficiency.

As you continue to perform this task consistently, the neural pathway becomes stronger and more defined in your brain—much like a well-trodden path through a forest. Over time, the routine activity becomes automatic, and you no longer need to think about it consciously—it's a habit.

Remember when you first learned to drive? Those first few lessons were likely filled with intense concentration, sweaty palms, and possibly some remarkable mistakes. Now, you likely navigate your daily commute with hardly a second thought. This is habit formation at work.

Research has also indicated that dopamine—a neurotransmitter linked with reward and motivation—plays a crucial role in habit formation. When we perform an action that results in a positive outcome, a dopamine spike reinforces the behavior. In the Habit Loop, rewards usually lead to the release of dopamine, making the individual more likely to repeat the behavior in the future.

Dopamine's role extends even further, however, as it begins to get released not just following the reward, but even in anticipation of it. This is why it's so hard to resist the temptation of unhealthy foods or other bad habits—we're not just enjoying the reward; we're getting a dopamine hit before we've even received it!

Therefore, dopamine enhances the stickiness of habits, both good and bad. It's one reason why harmful habits are so challenging to break and why rewarding good behavior can be very helpful in forming positive habits.

Research also suggests that, over time, the brain begins to anticipate rewards based on particular cues and therefore initiates the routine part of the habit loop. As a result, an external or internal cue alone can drive us into autopilot mode. Knowing this, we can be more conscious and deliberate about the cues we expose ourselves to, aiding us in forming beneficial habits or breaking destructive ones.

To sum up, habit formation results from the brain's inherent drive for efficiency and the neurochemical rewards that reinforce beneficial behaviors. Building awareness of these processes will equip you with a deeper understanding of your own habits, paving the way for adaptive changes in the service of your greater success. If we take advantage of this self-awareness and leverage it correctly, we're setting ourselves up for greater long-term achievement. Indeed, by better understanding why we do what we do, we can begin to change how we do things—and ultimately, who we become.

Strategies for Building and Breaking Habits

Our brains are constantly changing, forming new neural connections and pathways based on our daily experiences, thoughts, and behaviors. One counterintuitive, yet potent aspect of this ongoing process is habit formation. The reality is, habits, whether constructive or destructive, have a profound influence on our lives. Therefore, understanding how to build beneficial habits and break the harmful ones is an integral part of crafting a successful life.

Habits are essentially automatic responses to specific triggers in our environment. They are behaviors that we repeat so frequently they become almost unconscious. The brain, always looking for ways to save effort, begins to automate such recurring behavior patterns. This automation is where the real crux of a habit lays. It's not necessarily the behavior itself, but the mental shortcut the brain uses that is the habit.

So how can we leverage this understanding to build positive habits? The first step is identifying the desired behavior then link it with a specific trigger. This trigger will act as a cue to your brain to begin the automatic process. For instance, if you're trying to establish a habit of morning meditation, you could use a specific alarm tone as your trigger to remind you to meditate.

However, deciding to create a new habit and actually making it stick are two different matters. Persistence plays an essential role. Remember, repetition is the key. The more frequently you perform a behavior, the more ingrained the habit becomes, akin to carving a path through a dense forest. The first few times might be challenging, but eventually, walking the path becomes much more comfortable.

Another effective strategy for building habits is piggybacking on already established ones. This is often referred to as habit stacking. Basically, you connect your new desired habit with one you perform consistently. For example, if you want to start flossing daily and you're already in the habit of brushing your teeth every morning and night, try adding flossing to your tooth brushing routine.

Using rewards can also be beneficial. A reward offers a kind of 'immediate gratification' that can motivate you to persist even if the benefits of the habit aren't immediately apparent. Rewards could be something as simple as a five-minute break with a good book after finishing a significant task, or treating yourself to a favorite delicacy after an intense workout.

But what about breaking negative habits? The process of breaking habits mirrors that of building them. The first, and sometimes most challenging step, is becoming aware of the habit you wish to alter. For instance, suppose you have a habit of mindlessly scrolling social media before bedtime. In that case, the first step to breaking the habit is consciously recognizing when you reach for your phone.

Once the habit is identified, it's crucial to comprehend what triggers it. Perhaps it's boredom, stress, or a particular time of day. Mapping out your habit can be an excellent way to understand it and identify the best ways to break it.

Next, you need to design a new response to the trigger. It's almost impossible to delete a habit completely from our brains. Instead, replace the negative behavior with a positive one. For example, instead of reaching for your phone when you're bored, pick up a book or engage in a hands-on hobby.

Fostering accountability can be especially useful in breaking negative habits. This is because it introduces an external factor that boosts your motivation to stick to your commitments. You can share your goal with a trusted friend or family member, or even join a supportive group with similar objectives.

Lastly, nurturing patience and self-compassion is crucial. Change is rarely a straight path, and you will inevitably encounter setbacks. How you respond to these bumps along the way can be the difference between lapsing back into old patterns or pushing forward and successfully altering the habit.

In essence, understanding the mechanisms of habit formation and using strategic techniques—like identifying triggers, using rewards, habit stacking, and fostering accountability—can help you in creating beneficial habits and breaking harmful ones, ultimately leading you closer to your goals of success.

Consistency: The Key to Neural Reprogramming

Repetition is essential to building and sustaining habits, as we've discussed previously. This same principle is crucial in maintaining behavioral changes through neural reprogramming. Consistency is the means through which we can achieve this. The key aspect in this case is maintaining regular, consistent practice of the new behaviors and thought processes we're aiming to adopt.

Let's understand this further: When we look within our brains, we can see a mirrored practice of consistency. The more often a certain neural pathway is used, the stronger it becomes. Repetition solidifies the connection, making it easier for future electrical impulses to travel along. It's the entire foundation for learning and forming habits.

Let's consider the most basic form of learning, conditioned response. When we regularly pair a stimulus with a certain response, we ultimately condition our brains to respond that way automatically to that stimulus. This is no different when it comes to achieving success. By consistently aligning our actions and thoughts with those that breed success, we set a foundation for our minds to naturally produce such behaviors.

Consistency, however, is hard to maintain. Life is complex, busy, and unpredictable. Sticking to a routine or habit amidst such chaos presents a significant challenge. A part of our brains, indeed, thirsts for novelty and change. So, how do we manage to maintain habits in the face of such adversity?

Firstly, it's essential to set realistic and achievable goals. A sense of achievement is a powerful motivator, encouraging us to stay on track. Small victories, accumulated regularly, keep our confidence up and build momentum. Remember, it's not about making a massive change overnight. It's about taking small steps consistently. This in turn makes the desired changes become part of our routine, part of our neural programming.

Secondly, understand that consistency doesn't mean rigidity. It doesn't require you to solidly stick to the same routine day after tedious day. You can be consistent in your actions while maintaining some degree of flexibility. Adjust your plans as needed, but always make sure to stay aligned with your overall goals. Recognize that change is a natural part of life. Don't get frustrated with yourself if you have to adjust your schedule or tactics. Keep your eyes on the prize - the change you are striving for.

Thirdly, celebrate your progress. As we've mentioned in previous chapters, marking your milestones cultivates a sense of accomplishment, which can further reinforce the habit you're trying to establish. Recognize and reward consistency. Your brain will start to link the beneficial action with the positive feelings associated with accomplishment and reward.

The good news is, this is something that can be applied to any area of life. Whether you're looking to achieve financial success or improve personal relationships, you can apply consistency to reach those objectives. You need not be a prisoner to your past habits and thought processes. Through consistent practice, your brain will adapt and adjust, allowing you to reach your full potential.

To end, remember, don't expect instant results. The brain might be incredibly adaptive, but neural reprogramming isn't an overnight process. It might take weeks or even months of consistent effort before you start seeing changes.

But be assured, once those changes take hold, they are incredibly powerful. They become part of you and shape how you interact with the world.

So, hold on to consistency, whether in times of triumph or adversity. If you stay the course, you could find yourself embracing newer, healthier habits that can set you up for success. Keep your mind open to the beauty of small but consistent changes. They can indeed produce cascading effects, influencing not just your neural pathways, but your life as a whole.

Consistency, quite frankly, is the silent hero of neural reprogramming. Through our understanding of how habits form and how neural pathways strengthen, we can grasp the importance this steady, enduring application of effort plays in transforming our lives. It is through consistent practice and repetition that we encourage our brain to make long-lasting changes leading to greater success in our lives.

Next, we move onto understanding how our emotions play a significant role in achieving success, and what techniques we can use to harness them. So, be ready to dive deeper into your incredible, adaptable mind.

Chapter 7: Harnessing Emotions for Success

At this juncture, we've explored the vast power of the brain, examined the key elements of success, and delved into the mechanisms by which we form habits to achieve success. However, what hasn't been given its due attention yet is the crucial, complex, and often, misunderstood world of emotions and how they can be channeled for success. Being human involves experiencing a broad spectrum of emotions, and we mustn't dismiss or suppress them; instead, we should strategically harness these feelings. Emotional intelligence involves understanding your emotions, the emotions of people around you, and making decisions that consider both of these. Superior emotional intelligence fuels success by paving the path for improved decision-making, relationships, and personal well-being. Moreover, developing robust emotional regulation skills enables us to adapt to changing circumstances and navigate life's ups and downs with greater ease and resilience. Thus, when we learn to not simply react, but use emotions strategically in driving towards our purpose, we can turbocharge our path to success.

The Role of Emotions in Decision Making

Let's picture our emotions as the co-pilots of our decision-making journey. Every choice we make is influenced to some extent by our feelings - fear, joy, anger, anticipation, and countless others. They sit alongside the rational part of our mind, exerting their own subtle influence over the journey's direction.

Feelings offer a different kind of wisdom than reason. They can sometimes alert us to consequential factors that logic alone may overlook. Often, when we speak of 'going with our gut', we're referring to this emotional insight. It's as if your emotions are saying, "we can't fully explain it yet, but something important is happening here."

Emotions can motivate us to take action. Think, for example, of the surge of adrenaline that pushes you to work harder in a competition or the joy that keeps you committed to a beloved hobby. Achievements and victories often have an emotional catalyst.

However, emotions can also lead to biased or hasty decision making. When we're in the grip of strong emotion, we may overlook essential information, fail to consider the long-term consequences of our actions, or mistreat others in the heat of the moment. Irony is that, these are the decisions we often live to regret.

Our emotions also intertwine with our beliefs, attitudes, and perceptions, all of which color our view of the world. For instance, if you've been bitten by a dog as a child, you might feel fear and caution around all dogs, even the friendliest ones. That's your past emotional experience influencing your current decisions.

Furthermore, our moods can also impact our decisions. It's not uncommon to make more optimistic choices when we're in a good mood and more pessimistic ones when we're feeling glum. It's as if our emotions cast a filter over our reality, altering the world in accordance with their hue.

While all of this might make emotions seem capricious or problematic, they're actually not. They're simply a part of who we are. To dismiss emotions as irrational or unimportant is to dismiss an essential aspect of our humanity.

The key, then, isn't to try and suffocate our emotions, but rather to understand and harness them. One of the first steps toward this is recognizing that emotions, for all their flavors and intensities, are transitory. They pass and shift like weather patterns. They might cloud our judgement in one moment, only to illuminate wisdom the next.

Another crucial strategy is learning how to identify your emotions. Many of us are surprisingly bad at this. We can spin a vague sense of discomfort into a tale of looming disaster, or shrug off genuine joy as nothing important. Yet, recognizing and naming our emotions can help us understand their influence on our decisions.

Practicing mindfulness can help in this process. Mindfulness encourages us to step back and observe our emotions without judgment or reaction. It allows us to see how our feelings sway our thoughts and actions, offering valuable insight into our decision-making processes.

Mindfully responding to our emotions can help us navigate through difficult decision-making scenarios. It helps us to not be overwhelmed by stressful or immediate emotions; rather, it enables us to view them as passing internal events and respond to them from a calm and centered place.

Emotional self-regulation, too, is a crucial component of successful decision-making. It involves the ability to manage difficult emotions, and to summon positive emotions when needed. Emotional regulation makes it easier for us to make well-balanced decisions that align with our long-term goals and values.

Knowledge about our emotions and how to manage them effectively enables us to confidently assess situations, weigh pros and cons, and make decisions based on a balance of emotion and logic. This balance is key, as all-successful decision making involves a finely-tuned blend of both.

So, as you navigate through your journey towards personal improvement and success, remember emotions aren't your detractors but allies. When tuned properly, they create a symphony of wisdom that can guide you through the various nuances of life.

Emotional Intelligence and its Contribution to Success

Having explored the impact of emotions on decision-making in the previous section, it is crucial to delve deeper into how emotional intelligence or EI contributes to success. Emotional Intelligence is the ability to understand, manage and effectively express one's own emotions, as well as engage and navigate successfully with the emotions of others.

At the heart of emotional intelligence lies the principle of being in tune with your own and others' emotions. There's a lot more to success than simply being smart or hardworking. Emotions play a significant role in shaping our actions, decisions, and interactions. This is where emotional intelligence comes into play.

A person who possesses a high degree of emotional intelligence recognizes and comprehends their own emotions, and this self-awareness allows them to manage their feelings more effectively. When you know what you're feeling and why, you're in a better position to make decisions, communicate with others, and manage stress.

Now, what does empathy have to do with success? Well, empathy, or the ability to understand and share the feelings of others, is a core component of emotional intelligence. Empathy doesn't mean you have to agree with others or take on their emotions, but rather that you can understand and respect their feelings, furthering collaborations and relationships.

Moreover, emotionally intelligent people have a knack for relating to others. They're adept at discerning the emotional states of those around them, which grants them an uncanny ability to respond appropriately. This will pave the way for effective communication, better relationship management, and ultimately, a more cohesive and productive work environment or personal partnerships.

Also, emotional intelligence involves understanding and managing the relationship between your thoughts and your emotions. What few people realize is that our thoughts directly influence how we feel. This means that by being aware of your thought patterns and mindfully reframing negative or unhelpful thoughts, you can regulate your emotional state more efficiently.

Resilience is yet another facet of emotional intelligence. Resilience is the capacity to bounce back from setbacks and adapt to change. Emotionally intelligent people have a positive outlook on life which helps them see failures as stepping stones to success, not as a derailment from achieving their goals.

Furthermore, an understated aspect of emotional intelligence is the power of self-regulation. A person with a high EQ can control impulsive feelings and behaviors, manage emotions in healthy ways, and adapt to changing circumstances. This self-regulation promotes trustworthiness and consistency, both of which contribute to success.

Another key area of emotional intelligence is self-motivation. Emotionally intelligent individuals don't require external motivators to strive for success. Instead, they're driven by an inherent desire to achieve, setting goals for themselves and diligently working towards reaching them due to an inner drive.

Considering all the above, it's clear that emotional intelligence significantly contributes to success. From effective communication and relationship management to resilience, self-regulation, and intrinsic motivation, an individual with high emotional intelligence is poised to succeed in various aspects of life.

However, it's important to note that developing emotional intelligence is not an overnight task. It's a process that takes time and constant mindful effort. Cultivating emotional intelligence begins with acknowledging emotions - both in oneself and in others and learning to manage them towards creating a positive impact.

Ultimately, high emotional intelligence allows for greater self-monitoring, empathy, understanding others, and channeling emotions into effective and positive actions. By investing in your emotional intelligence, you're investing in a key to unlock a higher level of personal and professional success.

So, in the quest for success, we should not overlook the power of emotions. Cultivating emotional intelligence is like equipping oneself with a compass that navigates through the complex maze of interpersonal relationships, personal growth, and achievement. With the right tools and determination, one can harness the power of emotions to fuel their journey toward success.

With this understanding in mind, the subsequent chapter will provide techniques for emotional regulation and mastery, a crucial step towards enhancing your emotional intelligence.

Techniques for Emotional Regulation and Mastery

Learning to harness your emotions for success doesn't just mean acknowledging their existence. It requires learning techniques to regulate and even master these feelings. To achieve true NeuroSuccess, we must be able to manage our emotions, giving them the space they require without letting them completely control us. Let's take a look at a few powerful techniques for regulating and mastering our emotional responses.

One transformative technique lies in the well-established field of Cognitive Behavioral Therapy (CBT). CBT involves changing our thought habits leading to a shift in emotional responses. For example, If you're finding yourself getting overly stressed or frustrated at work, don't just ignore it, observe it! Ask yourself, "what's causing me to feel this way?" Then, challenge these thoughts, asking whether they're fully accurate or if they're worst-case assessments. By doing so, we can regulate our emotional responses to these situations.

Another profound concept in emotional regulation is Mindfulness, a form of meditation where you focus on being completely present in the moment. This allows you to identify and understand your feelings and emotions instead of simply reacting to them impulsively. The more you can witness your emotions before you react to them, the more control you'll gain over them. In time, you'll be able to respond in a balanced and thoughtful way, rather than simply reacting. It's a magnificent tool for emotional mastery.

Deep breathing is another simple but effective technique for emotional regulation. When we become emotional, our breath can often become fast and shallow. By consciously slowing and deepening our breaths, we can help calm our emotional state. It's a case of the body leading the mind, an aspect of biofeedback that's a beautiful testament to our brain's plasticity.

The act of journaling can also offer substantial support in managing emotions. Writing about your feelings can help process them and lessen their impact. It's like having a conversation with your emotions, listening to what they're trying to tell you, and responding in a balanced manner. Picture this as a dialogue between you and your emotions, rather than a monologue where your emotions steamroll over your logic and reason. This offers a chance to gain more control and mastery over your emotional responses.

Another pivotal tool at your disposal is what psychologists call 'disputing.' It involves challenging your emotional reactions by questioning their accuracy. For instance, imagine you're feeling guilty. Ask yourself, "is there a genuine reason for me to feel this way?" Frequently, you'll find that the guilt isn't justified and that allows for emotional regulation.

Mental rehearsals can hold great promise too. This involves visualizing different scenarios and regulating your emotional responses accordingly. So if you're worried about an upcoming presentation, visualize it taking place smoothly. This can help decrease negative emotions associated with the event. It's like a virtual reality practice, giving your mind a head-start for real-world encounters.

Emotional freedom techniques or 'tapping' could be beneficial as well. This process combines tapping on certain body parts while saying affirmations to help reduce the intensity of negative emotions. While it may seem unorthodox to some, numerous studies have shown its effectiveness in emotional regulation.

The power of self-soothing should not be under-appreciated either. Comforting yourself in times of intense emotions can help bring balance. This could be as simple as enjoying a cup of your favorite tea, taking a relaxing bath, or listening to calming music. Such activities serve to distract your brain from the emotional upheaval, giving you time to regain your composure.

Sometimes, regulating emotions can also involve physical activities. Yes, you've read it right! It could be as simple as going for a walk or doing some yoga. Physical exercises can help release pent-up emotions and relieve stress, regaining emotional equilibrium.

The practice of gratitude can be a potent tool for emotional regulation too. It involves focusing on the good aspects of your life, which has the effect of countering negative emotions. With time, you'll find that the habit of being grateful can significantly help in emotion management.

Maintaining a balanced lifestyle also plays a crucial role in emotional regulation. Eating a balanced diet, getting sufficient sleep, and indulging in regular physical activity all have a profound impact on our emotional well-being. Your brain, just like any machine, functions better when it's well-cared for.

Time management can also work wonders when it comes to emotional regulation. Being in control of your time can reduce feelings of stress and anxiety, leading to better emotional well-being. Minimize procrastination, prioritize necessary tasks, delegate when possible, and don't forget to take time for relaxation too.

As you try these techniques, remember that mastering emotional regulation is not an overnight process. It takes commitment and consistency. Also, it's okay to seek professional help when needed. Therapists and counselors are trained to help you navigate through the process of gaining emotional regulation and mastery. You are not alone in your journey towards NeuroSuccess. Each step you take brings you closer to a better emotional balance and subsequently, greater success.

Chapter 8: Strategic Learning and Memory Boosting

Learning is an integral part of your personal growth journey, and by leveraging certain strategies, you can significantly amplify its effects. Strategic learning isn't about the quantity of information consumed, rather, it's about the quality of the learning process and the ability to retain and apply this knowledge effectively. To boost your memory, a brain-friendly teaching approach called the 'spaced repetition' can be employed. This method involves learning in small chunks over time, allowing your brain to solidify connections and deepen memory recall. Developing mnemonic devices such as 'memory palaces', where you create vivid mental images and associate them with the information you're trying to remember, can also assist in retention. Leaning into brain-boosting habits such as regular mental exercise, good nutrition, and consistent sleep can help optimise your cognitive functions; these will be covered in depth in Chapter 10. Remember, education doesn't cease when regular schooling ends. Embracing lifelong learning, whether through formal education or targeted self-improvement, forms a vital key to your continued growth and success.

Brain-Boosting Techniques for Enhanced Learning

After understanding the powerful potentials of the brain and the varied aspects of neurosuccess, it's time to delve deeper into the techniques you can harness to enhance your learning capabilities. If you've ever wondered if you could learn faster, retain more information, and apply your knowledge more effectively, then you're in the right place. There are many scientifically-proven brain-boosting techniques that can enhance your learning, a few of which we will explore in this section.

The first technique to consider is **mind mapping**. A mind map is a visual representation of your thoughts and ideas. It's like a more interactive, more refined version of brainstorming. Not only does mind mapping help with memory retention and recall, but it also makes it easier for you to connect different concepts and ideas. This process allows you to graphically organize and analyze complex information in a way that the brain can process more efficiently.

Next up, we have the **Feynman Technique** - a technique named after physicist Richard Feynman, known for his ability to simplify complex ideas. It's a four-stage process: learning a concept, teaching it to someone (or pretending to do so), identifying gaps in your understanding, and reviewing the material until you can explain it in simple terms. This iterative method not only helps you deeply understand a topic but also helps to pinpoint the areas you need to improve upon.

Another technique for enhanced learning is to *divide and conquer*. Rather than attempting to digest an entire topic or book in a single gulp, break it down into smaller parts. This is the principle behind the concept of 'chunking'—a cognitive strategy for making more efficient use of short-term memory by grouping together. Long lists or large pieces of information are more easily remembered when they're segmented into bite-sized chunks.

Let's not underestimate the power of **active recall**. Unlike passive review, where we simply read or watch material, active recall requires you to recall and write down what you've learned without looking at your notes or book. Active recall strengthens neural connections, helping convert short-term memory into long-term memory.

If you've always wanted to remember names, lists, or even complex concepts with ease, *mnemonic devices* can come to your rescue. These are techniques we use to help our brains better encode and recall important information. They work by associating easy-to-remember constructs with lists of terms or concepts, using such tricks as acronyms, visualizations, or narratives.

Perhaps one of the more enjoyable ways to boost your brain's learning capacity is through the use of **music**. Music can impact various areas of cognition, including attention, memory, and mood. Classical music, in particular, is often cited as having beneficial effects on memory and focus. However, it's crucial to remember that everyone is different —if classical music is not your cup of tea, find what works for you.

Don't forget to give your brain the break it needs. *Rest and relaxation* are just as crucial as active learning periods. The neurobiological process that takes place during rest - known as consolidation - allows the brain to solidify what it has learned, moving information from short-term to long-term memory.

An important aspect of enhanced learning is also **focus**. Eliminating distractions, practicing mindfulness, and staying single-tasked are crucial to staying focused. Focus isn't just about the brain's capacity to pay attention to a single task; it's also very much about resisting irrelevant information.

You also might want to experiment with learning at different times of the day. Some people find that they're more attentive and able to absorb more information during *specific times of the day.* Identifying your peak learning times and scheduling your study sessions around them can enhance your ability to learn and retain information.

The principle of **interleaving** - the process of mixing up different types of problems or topics in one study session - can also be beneficial. This approach encourages the brain to discern between different types of information and apply the correct methods to solve problems, thereby enhancing the learning process.

Just as physical exercise keeps your body in top form, your mind also benefits from *cognitive exercises.* Tasks like puzzles, reading, writing, or learning a new language can help keep your brain sharp, facilitating neural plasticity, and improving cognition.

Your **diet and hydration** are also factors that contribute to brain-boosting. Eating a balanced diet that includes essential fatty acids, antioxidants, and B vitamins, and staying hydrated can enhance brain function, giving your brain the nutrition it needs to process and recall information efficiently.

Finally, *consistent repetition* is another robust technique for solidifying new memories and facilitating recall. Repetition strengthens the neural pathways our brains use to connect and retrieve information, helping us learn and remember over the long term.

Indeed, boosting your brain's learning capacity isn't a one-size-fits-all formula. It's about trying different techniques, understanding what works best for you, and remembering that changing and evolving your strategies as you grow and change is not just okay—it's beneficial! After all, your brain is as unique as you are. These techniques are the tools in your toolbox, waiting to help you build your path to enhanced learning and success. So why not give them a try?

Memory Palaces and Other Mnemonic Devices

Highlighting the extraordinary capabilities of your brain, let's discuss a distinct series of brain-training techniques. These are called mnemonic devices. Mnemonic devices are techniques people use to help them improve their ability to remember something. They're always used in teaching and training to make learning more efficient, and one of the most effective mnemonic techniques is known as the Method of Loci, or the Memory Palace.

The Memory Palace technique is a method of memory enhancement which uses visualizations of familiar spatial environments in order to enhance the recall of information. The idea is simple. Picture yourself walking through a place you know well, for example, your house. Within this imagined setting, you strategically place the items or bits of information you're trying to remember.

The effectiveness of the Memory Palace technique is due in part to the human brain's ability to recall images and spatial detail more effectively than mere words or concepts. By associating abstract information with vivid, personal visuals, the data becomes more meaningful, and thus, easier to recall. This process is called encoding.

Here is how you can build a memory palace. First, identify a familiar space—your house, your office, a favorite park. Next, mentally walk through the space identifying various locations easy to visualize. Place one piece of information in each location. Replay the walk in your mind, focusing on each piece of information. It is vital to create vivid, colorful, unusual or even bizarre images as these tend to stick in the mind better than mundane ones.

Another key to successfully using a memory palace is rehearsal. Walk through your memory palace frequently to strengthen your mental imagery and reinforce the information. Just as a muscle weakens without regular exercise, your memory too can lose its potency without frequent use.

Mnemonic devices aren't limited to spatial memory techniques. Rhymes, acronyms, and acrostics are all examples of mnemonic tools that can be used for memory training. Let's take acronyms, for instance. In school, you might have used the acronym HOMES to remember the names of the Great Lakes: Huron, Ontario, Michigan, Erie, and Superior.

Rhymes and songs can also prove to be effective mnemonic devices. You can probably relate to this from a young age when the alphabet song helped distinguish and remember 26 unique letters. Or perhaps you remember learning the order of operations in mathematics using the mnemonic 'Please Excuse My Dear Aunt Sally' (Parentheses, Exponents, Multiplication and Division, Addition and Subtraction).

Now, why are such mnemonic strategies so effective? This effectiveness can be attributed to the way our brains are wired. Studies show that our brain is overwhelmingly visual, meaning we easily remember objects, colors, and images. By visualizing, making associations, and linking them with different visual imagery or sounds, we can significantly enhance information recall.

These memory techniques aren't simply about cramming for tests or impressing friends. In the greater scheme of things, they can foster lifelong learning and intellectual growth. By capitalizing on the innate potential of our brain, we can become more adept at learning new languages, acquiring new skills, and assimilating complex bodies of knowledge.

Moreover, even if we are not gearing up to become memory champions, regular practice of these mnemonic techniques can help maintain cognitive health, contributing to brain longevity. Regularly challenging our brain with these techniques can help build new neuronal connections, strengthening the neural network and improving overall cognitive abilities.

So, don't underestimate the power of these simple mnemonic techniques. Integrated into our daily lives, they can bring about powerful transformations in how we learn and remember. By training our memory, we are ultimately training our brain, and a well-trained mind paves the path to success.

The key takeaway? Success is in your grasp, and the journey there needn't be daunting. By harnessing the extraordinary capabilities of your brain and engaging in strategic memory enhancement methods like the Memory Palace and other mnemonic devices, you'll find yourself well on your way to achieving your goals and witnessing your own NeuroSuccess.

Lifelong Learning: The Key to Continued Growth

In our journey towards success, commitment to lifelong learning is the linchpin that unlocks continued growth. Once we have developed an understanding of our brain's complex functionalities and imbued our lives with positive habits and emotional intelligence, we need to ensure we continue to evolve. That's where the commitment to being an eternal student comes in.

Lifelong learning is the continuous, voluntary, and self-motivated pursuit of knowledge for personal or professional reasons. It enhances our understanding of the world around us, provides us with better opportunities to overcome life's challenges, and ultimately equips us to lead a more fulfilling and successful life.

Why is lifelong learning significant, you might ask? Even as the world evolves, the desire for self-improvement persists. Understanding the impact of everyday decisions on cognitive function doesn't stop in a year or two. It's a lifetime journey. The world doesn't stop changing, and neither should we. By consistently learning, we can adapt to changes and remain relevant, enhancing our ability to achieve our goals.

Embrace learning new things in everyday experiences. Be it a conversation with a friend, reading a book, or even stumbling upon a new concept in a movie, inspiration and knowledge can come from anywhere. Each experience, each interaction, adds another layer to our understanding of the world around us. Remember, no knowledge is wasted.

Lifelong learning encourages curiosity. When you're consistently seeking out new knowledge, you're building a habit of curiosity. Questions lead to answers, which in turn spark new questions. This ongoing cycle fosters cognitive growth and can enhance critical thinking skills and problem-solving abilities.

Keeping an open mind is vital for lifelong learning. Learning is a two-way street, and the ability to accept new concepts, ideas and criticism is just as important as acquiring knowledge. Open-mindedness allows you to see the world from a wider perspective and consider different viewpoints, boosting emotional intelligence and understanding.

Remember, learning doesn't need to be a solo activity. Learning with others allows for the sharing of ideas, which can significantly enhance comprehension and retention. Tapping into the power of active participation and interaction introduces diversity and multidimensional thinking into your learning process.

Choose to be a lifelong learner and you're choosing to keep your brain active. Active learning, where you actively engage the material, has been shown to stimulate neuroplasticity, reinforcing the connections between brain cells and maintaining cognitive agility.

How can we infuse lifelong learning into our lives? It starts with nurturing a mindset of exploration and curiosity. Embrace change, challenge yourself regularly, and value the process of learning as much as the outcome. Learning is not merely confined to academic or professional training; it is about embedding a quest for knowledge in every aspect of life.

Find avenues that ignite your passion. Any subject that intrigues you is a potential magnet for gaining comprehensive knowledge. Whether it be painting, gardening, cooking, or coding, passion fuels engagement, making the learning journey fun and rewarding.

When you encounter information that contradicts what you know, rather than automatically dismissing it, delve into it. Engaging with opposing views will deepen your knowledge and give you a well-rounded perspective. This ability to balance multiple points view is extremely valuable in decision making, problem solving, and critical thinking.

A potential downside of lifelong learning is information overload. With the internet at our fingertips, vast amounts of knowledge and resources can feel overwhelming. Prioritize quality over quantity and focus on a few areas of interest rather than trying to consume all available information.

Finally, otivate yourself with progressive achievement. Setting learning goals and tracking your progress may keep you motivated. Choose a learning route that breaks down large end-goals into achievable units, allowing you to appreciate your progress and remain motivated in your journey of lifelong learning.

In conclusion, lifelong learning is more than a concept; it's a lifestyle. It is the center of personal growth, professional success, and fulfillment. The thirst for knowledge, combined with the willingness to put in the effort, harbingers a constantly evolving self. As we keep learning, we keep growing. And as we grow, we get one step closer to achieving fulfilling success.

Chapter 9: The Role of Relationships in NeuroSuccess

After developing a profound understanding of strategic learning and memory-boosting techniques in the previous chapter, it's pivotal to direct our attention towards the significant role of relationships in achieving NeuroSuccess. Relationships provide a social backdrop that plays an instrumental role in influencing our mindsets, emotions, and behaviors. The human brain is an inherently social organ; our neural connections are shaped and re-shaped by our interactions with others. Building powerful networks isn't simply a professional necessity, it's also beneficial for our brain's plasticity. A diverse and supportive network promotes increased cognitive diversity and resilience, enhancing our emotional intelligence, including capabilities such as empathy and compassion, vital components of success. Additionally, navigating through conflicts in relationships contributes to our cognitive and emotional flexibility. NeuroSuccess, therefore, entails fostering positive relationships that facilitate neural growth and equipping ourselves with the necessary social skills for managing interpersonal challenges. Emphasizing the development of relationship skills can provide the necessary social stimulus that our brains crave, encouraging faster and more efficient neural reprogramming towards success.

Building Powerful Networks for Success

We've covered a lot of ground so far on our journey, and now we're about to embark on a fundamental aspect of success – building powerful networks. Your brain is a network of neurons, constantly connecting and communicating. In the same vein, successful individuals build networks of relationships where each connection facilitates another — a network of allies, advisors, and advocates. Let's delve into the art and science of building powerful networks for success.

As human beings, we're wired for social connection. We thrive in communities, develop through interactions, and together, we create a collective brainpower. Being part of a network enhances your capacity to gather ideas, expose yourself to new opportunities, and even accelerate the success of your endeavors. Our networks are essentially extensions of our brain, and so cultivating a strong, beneficial network boosts not just your social well-being, but your intellect and capacity for success as well.

Comprehending the power of networks starts by understanding that no one accomplishes anything truly extraordinary alone. Behind every successful person is a web of relationships, a system of support and a network ripe with resources and opportunities. Your network is your net worth, as the saying goes. This isn't to quantify the value of relationships in monetary terms, but to recognize the significance of relationships and connections in shaping personal and professional growth.

Effective networking, however, isn't about mere transactional relationships. It's not just about who you know but how you engage with them. This differentiates a network from a community. Communities foster mutual support, while a network facilitates the exchange of information, ideas, and challenges.

Building a powerful network begins with your mindset. If you see networking merely as a means to an end, your efforts are likely to fall flat. Genuine networking is built on a foundation of curiosity, generosity, and authenticity. It's about understanding and appreciating the unique strengths, knowledge, and experiences each person brings to the table. It's less about what you can gain, and more about what you can learn, contribute, and share.

You must first understand that the strength of your network lies in its diversity. A diverse network brings a wealth of viewpoints, experiences, and skills that can potentially spark innovation and provide comprehensive solutions. Diversity in a network enhances creativity, fosters resilience, and widens the scope of opportunities.

Now, where do you start if you're looking to build a network? Start with those around you. Family, friends, neighbors, colleagues, and even casual acquaintances can all be part of your network. From here, finding common interests with others, be it through professional communities, clubs, online platforms, or mutual connections, is a gateway to expanding your network.

It's essential to understand, however, that building a network is not a one-and-done affair. It requires you to consistently nurture these connections through sharing, helping, and engaging. Remember, a network is a social contract where each party contributes. Give before you take. Establish yourself as a reliable, helpful, and empathetic individual in the network.

Effective networking also necessitates excellent communication skills. Learning to listen actively, express your ideas clearly, ask thoughtful questions, and show genuine interest in others is vital. Remember, it's not about dominating conversations but facilitating meaningful dialogues. The aim should be to learn, contribute, and build connections organically.

Beyond expanding your network, it's equally crucial to maintain the connections. This involves regular interactions, consistent value contribution, and mutual growth. Relationships that are not nurtured over time weaken, closing off valuable channels of knowledge and opportunities.

As we've learnt, a strong network aligns closely with neurological growth. It keeps your cognitive skills sharp, enhances problem-solving abilities, and supplies a steady stream of new insights and inspiration. As with neural connections in your brain, the more you exercise your networks, the stronger they become.

In conclusion, building powerful networks for success entails fostering meaningful connections with a broad range of people and drawing strength from these diversified relationships. It requires authenticity, diligence, and the right mindset. With a powerful network, you're not just enriching your personal life but significantly stretching the bounds of your potential for achieving success.

Starting today, expand your comfort zone, authentically reach out, and connect. Your powerful network awaits, together weaving a web that provides support, inspiration, and most importantly, success.

In the next section, we will explore the role of empathy, compassion, and their contribution to success. Stay tuned for this enlightening deeper dive into the role of social emotional intelligence within our journey towards NeuroSuccess.

Empathy, Compassion, and Success

In pursuing success, certain qualities are often overlooked. Empathy and compassion may seem unrelated to achievement, but they play a significant role in the journey toward success. Let's delve into the implications and implementations of these traits in this journey.

Social beings by nature, humans thrive within a community. And by affirming this, we must note that empathy, the ability to understand the feelings of others, can be the bridge to profound connections. In the realm of success, constructing solid relationships brings you closer to your goals.

By empathizing with your colleagues, employees, partners, or bosses, you can gain insight into their perspectives, motivations, and challenges. This comprehension fosters mutual respect, minimizes conflicts, promotes clearer cooperation, and ultimately boosts team productivity.

Notably, empathy strikes a significant influence on leadership. Effective leaders are those who can sympathize with their team, creating an environment wherein their subordinates feel understood and valued. This results in a motivated workforce, driving the group toward collective success.

Moving hand in hand with empathy is compassion. Being empathetic refers to emotionally connecting with another's experience, while being compassionate is feeling the desire to aid in alleviating someone else's suffering. Each trait enhances the other, fostering a healthier social bond.

A compassionate individual projects positivity, kindness, and support – values that inspire others. Imagine building your network around people who feel valued and supported by you. That is a powerful element promoting success. It not only encourages harmonious interaction but also propels cooperation, collaboration, and collective achievement.

Now, the question arises on how to cultivate empathy and compassion. These traits don't magically appear but can be enhanced through practice. For instance, active listening helps you become more empathetic. Don't merely hear the words - try to absorb the message and the emotions conveyed.

The practice of mindfulness plays a crucial role as well. Being present and wholly attentive to the current moment promotes empathic responses. Mindfulness encourages you not just to register the feelings of others but to genuinely understand and connect with them.

In contrast, compassion may seem natural to some people, but for others, it can be a learned ability. To nurture this trait, indulge in compassion reflection - think about a situation that required a compassionate response and reflect on how you or someone responded. Learning from these situations can help habituate the behavior.

Another powerful move to foster compassion is to look past your personal agenda and biases and view the world through an unbiased eye. By leveling the field and viewing everyone as inherently equal, you'll get the essence of true compassion.

Awareness of our shared humanity also fosters compassion. Recognizing that we're all made of the same cloth, albeit stitched differently, encourages understanding of others' trials, tribulations, and triumphs. Esteeming our shared experiences underlines the essence of compassion.

In a nutshell, infusing empathy and compassion into your life can escalate your movement towards success. Not only does it improve your relationships, but they also serve as invaluable leadership tools for managing teams and taskforces.

If you cultivate these qualities, you'll find that your path to achievement is smoother, more humane, and far more rewarding. However, note that these practices might not come naturally to you, but with deliberate mindfulness and reflection, you can foster empathy and compassion within you, improving your chances of success.

In our quest for success, let's keep in mind that empathy and compassion are not just 'nice-to-have' qualities. They are essential, and their role in our success story is pivotal. Embrace these traits, understand their power, and use them to propel you towards success.

Conflict Resolution and the Brain

Having examined in previous chapters the roles that emotions, habit formation, and relationships play in your success, we now turn our attention to an essential aspect of relationships: conflict resolution. Not only does it play a critical role in building and maintaining relationships, but it can also significantly impact your neural health and success levels.

Well-documented research has demonstrated the physiological effects conflict can have on the brain. In response to highly stressful scenarios, our bodies release cortisol, a hormone that readies us to respond to perceived threats, commonly known as the fight or flight response.

Cortisol isn't evil per se; it equips us to deal with immediate peril. But when our body's cortisol levels remain high due to ongoing stress or anxiety - such as that induced by unresolved conflict - it can have detrimental effects on our brain's health and functioning. It impedes our ability to process information, solve problems effectively, and even impacts our memories, and creativity - all elements important to achieving success.

That's why equipping yourself with the skills to peacefully resolve conflicts is not just essential for fostering strong, effective relationships but also for enhancing your neural function and moving toward NeuroSuccess.

To handle conflict effectively, we must first understand the impact it has on our brains. As previously mentioned, when conflict arises, it triggers a stress response that releases cortisol. This response, while useful in short-term dangerous situations, impairs cognitive functions crucial for conflict resolution such as active listening, empathy, and strategic problem-solving.

Imagine finding a middle ground or navigating a tricky negotiation when your short-term memory is lagging, or you can't think clearly. Add heightened emotions to the mix, and you have a recipe for further misunderstanding and escalating conflict.

In learning to manage conflict, it becomes pertinent to engage the prefrontal cortex, the brain's center for rational thought and the sector that gets adversely affected during stressful situations. So, in essence, conflict resolution involves managing stress responses to ensure they don't compromise our brain's high-level functions.

Effective conflict resolution involves three primary techniques: active listening, empathy, and problem-solving. These can't merely be turned on like a switch, they require practice and consistent effort to be effective, especially amidst conflict when stress hormones are running high.

The first step - active listening - is about giving undivided attention to understand the other party's perspective fully. It involves picking up the context and nuances of their point of view without allowing your emotions and stress responses to cloud your judgment. This mechanism activates neural pathways associated with understanding narratives and storylines, and can potentially promote empathy.

Empathy, the ability to understand and share the feelings of others, involves more than just acknowledging another's emotions - it requires feeling with them. It requires activating our mirror neurons, brain cells that activate when we observe another's action or emotion, allowing us to 'mirror' their experience in our brains and creating a sense of shared experience.

Problem-solving represents the third element of effectively resolving conflict. Successfully navigating this step hinges on the successful execution of the first two steps - active listening encourages understanding, and empathy promotes emotional resonance. With these in place, our stress responses are better managed, and productive problem-solving becomes possible.

In essence, implementing these conflict resolution strategies effectively helps to decrease our body's stress response, reducing cortisol levels, and facilitating increased cognitive functioning. As your brain adapts to these new ways of handling conflict, you solidify neural pathways involved in listening, empathy, and problem-solving, further empowering your capability for resolving disputes.

What's more, these skills don't just help overcome conflict in interpersonal relationships; they also come in handy when dealing with internal conflicts that emerge from self-doubt, fear or procrastination. By effectively managing these internal conflicts, you further your journey towards NeuroSuccess.

Thus, conflict resolution is far more than just a tool to quell disputes—it's a skill that, when effectively mastered, underpins our neural health, our relationships, and ultimately, our success. So let's remember, conflict isn't necessarily detrimental—it's how we choose to handle it that determines its impact.

Chapter 10: Maintaining Brain Health for Optimal Performance

Now that we've harvested insights about our neurological patterns and embarked on a journey to train our brain for success, let's dive deep into the realm of maintaining brain health as a vitally important ingredient in our NeuroSuccess strategy. While our brain is a complex and intricate organ with the power to shape our lives, it requires particular care and maintenance for optimal performance. First off, nutrition plays a critical role in our brain's health. Just as a high-performance car runs best on premium fuel, our brains function effectively when they're nourished with quality, nutrient-dense foods. Therefore, a diet rich in brain-boosting foods like berries, oily fish, broccoli, and turmeric can bolster cognitive function. Concurrently, there's a staggering amount of research indicating the profound effect of physical exercise on cognitive enhancement. Regular physical activity increases blood flow to your brain and helps stimulate the growth of new brain cells, improving your memory and thinking skills. Lastly, let's not overlook the undeniable importance of sleep. It's during sleep that your brain cleans out toxins, solidifies memories, and recharges for a new day. Adequate and quality sleep is paramount to brain health. Moreover, maintaining a healthy brain not only keeps cognitive decline at bay but also sets the stage for continued NeuroSuccess in your journey towards personal and professional growth.

Nutrition for the Brain

After understanding the foundations of success and the role that our minds play in building them, it's time for a deep dive into maintaining brain health with a particular focus on nutrition. Food isn't just fuel for the body. It's fuel for the brain too, and what you eat can significantly influence your cognitive abilities, mood, and energy levels - all vital aspects of achieving NeuroSuccess.

At the core of brain health is a balanced diet. Much like every cell in our body, the brain's perfect functioning needs a wide variety of nutrients. Notably, carbohydrates, particularly complex ones, serve as our brain's primary energy source. These include whole grains, fruits, and vegetables that provide a steady and reliable supply of glucose without the spikes and dips associated with processed sugars.

Proteins also play a significant role in brain health. They contain amino acids, which are vital for neurotransmitter synthesis and function. Lean meats, dairy, eggs, and plant-based proteins like lentils and nuts are excellent sources of these amino acids, acting as the building blocks for crucial chemicals like dopamine and serotonin - pivotal for maintaining motivation and a positive mindset.

Fats can't be overlooked when considering brain nutrition, but it's important to distinguish between different types. The brain is notably high in fats, especially omega-3 fatty acids, which aid in building cell membranes and have anti-inflammatory properties. Healthy sources include fatty fish, flax seeds, and walnuts.

Vitamins and minerals are essential too. For instance, B vitamins help produce energy, maintain the nervous system, and even aid in producing mood-enhancing chemicals. Good sources include leafy greens, whole grains, and animal products. Similarly, zinc and magnesium, found in nuts, lean meats, and whole grains, are essential for nerve signaling

Now, while the above pointers provide a general roadmap, it's clear that one size does not fit all when it comes to nutrition. Genetic differences, lifestyles, and health conditions can all influence how our bodies process nutrients.

Understanding your individual nutritional needs is crucial. For instance, it's well known that conditions like ADHD, depression, and Alzheimer's have been linked to specific nutritional deficiencies or imbalances. Acknowledging such unique nutritional needs can lead to tailored dietary choices that support optimal brain function.

Well-timed nutrition plays a vital role too. A steady meal schedule helps maintain stable blood sugar levels, steering away from energy slumps that can harm focus and motivation. Regularly spaced meals and snacks consisting of high-quality proteins, complex carbohydrates, and beneficial fats can boost cognitive performance.

Hydration also forms a key component of brain nutrition. The human brain comprises about 75% water, and even minor dehydration can impair focus, memory, and mood. The key is not just to drink when thirsty but maintain consistent hydration, ideally through plain water.

But nutritional hazards exist too. Excessive consumption of saturated fats, trans fats, and processed sugars can harm cognitive health, affecting memory, understanding, and mood. Negatively affecting neural health, these constitute barriers to NeuroSuccess. So, awareness and moderation of these substances are critical.

Nutritional supplementation is recommended where the required nutrients from food might be deficient. But, it's crucial to avoid the pitfall of considering supplements as replacements for a healthy diet. They're meant to complement, not substitute.

Eating for brain health does not merely imply a focus on physical food consumption. Mindful eating habits can enhance the nutritional experience. Slowing down to enjoy food can help manage stress, improve digestion, and bring a sense of satisfaction that could discourage overeating.

In conclusion, brain nutrition is not about stringent dietary rules or extreme restrictions. It's about understanding the science and making informed, balanced choices that boost brain health. The impact of these choices on your cognitive function, motivation, and overall wellbeing can be profound.

Remember, every meal is an opportunity to nourish your brain. By making proper nutritional choices, you can fuel your brain optimally, giving it the best support to rewire itself towards NeuroSuccess.

But brain health isn't solely based on nutrition. As we move into the next chapter, we'll dive into another significant factor - exercise, showcasing its role in cognitive enhancement, ultimately paving a concrete path towards all-encompassing brain health.

The Role of Physical Exercise in Cognitive Enhancement

As we delve deeper into the myriad ways of achieving and maintaining optimal brain health for success, it's necessary to underscore the impressively significant role physical exercise plays in cognitive enhancement. It's about stretching beyond what one initially thought was possible.

It's not just about achieving a fit body; physical exercise paves a path for enhancing your brain's fitness too.

Many people may wonder why physical fitness matters when our goal is mental transformation. In order to understand this, we must acknowledge a simple truth; our bodies and brains are intricately connected. What we do to our bodies impacts our brains. This lends credence to the age-old adage that states, "A sound mind resides in a sound body."

For years, scientists and health experts have sung praises about the benefits of exercise for the body - from maintaining a healthy weight, boosting the immune system, to promoting heart health. However, numerous studies in recent years have demonstrated that regular physical exercise can also enhance cognitive abilities such as memory, attention, and problem-solving skills.

Research shows that physical exercise increases the heart rate, which in turn pumps more oxygen to the brain. With better oxygen flow, our brains tend to function more effectively. However, the benefits don't just stop at improved oxygenation.

Physical activity stimulates the production of hormones in the brain that nourish and stimulate the growth of brain cells. This process is called Neurogenesis, which fundamentally impacts our brains' adaptability or plasticity as discussed in the previous chapters.

Exercise also boosts the secretion of endorphins, the body's natural mood elevators. These chemicals act as a form of natural antidepressant that can be produced within the body. Ensuring a regular flow of endorphins can go a long way in improving one's mood and emotional stability, aiding greatly in reaching our goals.

In addition, exercise can also stimulate brain regions that are involved in memory function to release a chemical called brain-derived neurotrophic factor (BDNF). BDNF rewires memory circuits so they work better. Think of it as the brain's personal trainer helping you to remember experiences and information effectively.

Therefore, consistent exercise can result in improved memory and thinking skills, protecting thinking skills and memory. In fact, research has shown an increase in volume in certain areas of the brain that control thinking and memory after a constant exercise regimen.

A variety of exercises can work effectively to enhance cognitive abilities. Aerobic exercises, like jogging, swimming, or dancing, have been shown to have significant impacts on brain health as they improve blood and oxygen flow to the brain. But, strength training and flexibility exercises also have their positive impacts. It's not about picking one activity over the other, but figuring out a balanced routine that works for you.

Maintaining a routine is crucial here. You can't expect to see an immediate transformation after one intense workout session. Instead, the key lies in consistency. Just like how a river cuts through a rock, not due to its power but persistence, it is our regular attempts at physical exercise that yield fruitful results.

Moreover, exercise provides an excellent outlet for alleviating stress which often interferes with effective cognitive performance. By providing a means of relaxation and detachment from every day's worries, physical exercise allows us to bring forth our best cognitive performance.

Regular physical exercise can result in a ripple effect of health benefits for both the body and the brain. It's not merely an activity that you squeeze into your schedule if you get the time, but rather an essential element that can propel your journey towards success. Hence, don't consider exercise as a chore, but an opportunity to enhance your mental prowess and thus inch closer to your goals.

So as you move ahead in this journey, start thinking about how you can integrate regular physical exercise into your Regimen. The initial step might seem like a big jump, but the more you push yourself to maintain the routine, the more natural and enjoyable it would become!

Moving forward, let's examine another vital aspect of maintaining brain health for optimal performance: Sleep and its importance. Rest assured, it's more significant than you might have imagined!

Sleep and its Undeniable Importance

We've touched upon various aspects of maintaining brain health for optimal performance in our journey so far, discussing nutrition and physical exercise in detail. Now, it's time to dive deep into one aspect that is often neglected but which is of paramount importance - sleep. We can't stress enough how much of a role a good night's sleep plays in your overall neurohealth, and by extension, your journey to NeuroSuccess.

Understanding and acknowledging the importance of sleep goes beyond just knowing that it makes you feel good the next day. The actual role sleep performs is far more multifaceted and intricate. Think of sleep as the brain's default maintenance system that operates 'under the hood' to ensure smooth functioning.

Scientific research has increasingly revealed that sleep is vital for our brains to consolidate and process memories from the day. Without enough sleep, we can struggle to remember, concentrate, and stay sharp, thus barring us from operating at our optimum cognitive capabilities. This has a cascading effect on our potential to succeed.

What happens when you don't get enough sleep? Neural connections that form memory become frazzled, and our ability to make clear decisions, manage emotions and maintain a steady mood becomes compromised. Furthermore, chronic sleep deprivation makes us susceptible to an array of health concerns such as obesity, diabetes, depression, and heart disease. It's clear that lack of sleep can be a major roadblock on your path to NeuroSuccess.

So, how can one improve their sleep? Well, let's start with the basics. You should aim for a minimum of seven to nine hours of sleep per night. Consistency matters, too. Going to sleep and waking up at the same time every day, even on weekends, helps to set a regular sleep schedule.

But it's not just about the number of hours. Quality of sleep matters too. A restful sleep involves several stages, including the crucial REM (Rapid Eye Movement) stage, which is where a lot of the brain's heavy rejuvenation and processing work happens. Ensuring a sleep environment that aids these stages is important. A quiet, dark, and cool bedroom is generally most conducive to good sleep.

It's also worth examining your sleep habits, also known as sleep hygiene. This includes habits like winding down before bed, keeping electronics away from the bedroom, and avoiding caffeine and nicotine close to bedtime. Some people find that including a relaxing activity, such as reading or meditating, into their nighttime routine helps prepare their brain for sleep.

Exercising regularly and maintaining a healthy diet stimulated with lots of fruits, vegetables, lean proteins and whole grains also favor quality sleep. You may also want to consider cutting down, if not completely eliminating alcohol, as it interferes with your sleep cycles and prevents restful sleep.

Now you might wonder, "What if I have trouble sleeping despite maintaining good sleep hygiene?". This is where it might be useful to seek professional advice. Sleep disorders such as insomnia, sleep apnea and restless leg syndrome can disrupt your sleep and lead to chronic sleep deprivation. If you're suffering from such a condition, it's important to address it with your healthcare provider.

A common mindset shared by many high-performers is the 'sleep is for the weak' mentality. This mindset needs to shift. It's counterproductive and objectively untrue. In fact, powerful leaders, from elite athletes to successful entrepreneurs, have attributed considerable portions of their success to quality sleep.

Apart from the practical aspects of improving and respecting sleep, it's crucial to adopt a mindset that sees sleep not as an inconvenience or timewaster, but as an essential element for high performance and mental clarity. Only then can you harness the power of sleep for optimum neurohealth.

Incorporating quality, restful sleep as a non-negotiable in your routine can bolster your neural health like nothing else. This, coupled with the strategies for brain health, personal development and success we've discussed so far in this journey, places you firmly on a path of long-term and sustainable NeuroSuccess.

In the subsequent sections, we'll delve into real-life case studies that demonstrate how all these components come together. We'll analyze the stories of individuals who have overcome adversity and achieved incredible things by harnessing the principles of NeuroSuccess. But before we go there, let's re-emphasize the critical role that sleep plays in your journey to NeuroSuccess - it's quite literally the foundation on which we build the rest of our success strategies.

Chapter 11: Case Studies: Real-life Stories of NeuroSuccess

In this chapter, we'll delve into several life-altering instances where the methods and teachings highlighted in the preceding chapters were brought into real-world application. First, let's examine the significant shift in the life of a poverty-stricken individual who harnessed the power of neural transformation to achieve success beyond the imaginable. This case exemplifies the profound impact a positive mindset, neural reprogramming, and consistent efforts have on materializing one's dreams. Next, we will study some inspiring tales of resilience, focusing on individuals who have faced and surmounted seemingly insurmountable adversities. These stories underscore the potency of emotional mastery, fear management, and overcoming procrastination, thus demonstrating that irrespective of your present circumstances, NeuroSuccess is possible and attainable.

From Rags to Riches: The Power of Neural Transformation

Success, in its true essence, is not a destination but a journey. It's about transforming one's life, rewriting narratives, and shaping a new reality. We often view success as a tangible thing that we strive to reach, but in most cases, it's an intangible process from rags to riches. By 'rags', we aren't merely referring to financial struggles; the term includes mental roadblocks, self-doubts, fear, and procrastination. 'Riches' denotes not only wealth, but also peace of mind, self-certainty, courage, persistence, and accomplishments.

Every rich after rags story begins with a 'neural transformation'. You've seen it in those who have overcome tremendous hardships to achieve phenomenal success. You might have wondered how they managed such remarkable transformations. They all started with the basic understanding that the brain is immensely adaptable and its potential, unbounded.

The neuroscience of success elucidates that a growth mindset, strong belief system, resilience, optimism, and discipline can rewire our brains for success. This 'neural transformation', though not an overnight process, can lower the barriers to success, infuse energy, and expand the horizon of possibilities.

At the root of this transformation is brain plasticity, as discussed in previous chapters. The ability of the brain to change and adapt over time lets us hone new skills, build resilience, and bolster our determination. When we persistently engage in healthy thought patterns, positive self-talk, visualization techniques, and mindfulness, we 'retrain' the brain to be more success-oriented.

One remarkable case that perfectly captures the power of neural transformation is the story of a homeless man who braved the severe weather conditions of New York City to become a renowned computer programmer. His hardships never made him bitter, but only more determined. Mindset was his tool for purging his brain of negativity and filling it with hope, perseverance, and dedication.

His transformation was rooted in the belief that his current state didn't define his capabilities or future. He replaced thoughts of despair with affirmation of success, practiced visualization, and embraced learning. By persisting to learn programming through makeshift cardboard computers, he instilled new patterns and pathways in his brain that bolstered his belief in his potential and raised his chances of success.

Feeding the brain with optimism, resilience, motivation, and passion can take us leaps and bounds towards our goals. When we listen to and believe in the silently whispered affirmations of our subconscious, our minds become the breeding ground for success.

In another illustrative instance, a woman - a victim of domestic violence - overcame her trauma to become an influential speaker. Her journey of transformation began with overcoming the victim mentality and adopting a survivor's mindset. Through the power of neurotransformation, she learned to use her past experiences for growth.

She harnessed emotion regulation techniques to see past her traumas and used her hardship as a stepping stone to greater achievement. By nurturing positive emotions and persistently seeking to move ahead, she modified her brain's emotional responses. Today, she uses her experience and acquired knowledge to inspire others to bounce back from adversity.

Similarly, individuals across various socio-economic backgrounds have risen above their circumstances by utilizing the power of neural transformation. Their stories of perseverance and triumph are a testament to the brain's astonishing ability to reshape itself for success.

As we gleaned from these stories, enhancing our neural pathways and thought patterns is within our control. With consistent efforts, we can redefine our responses to situations, transform our expectations, and in turn, shape our realities.

Neural transformation doesn't end once we attain our goals. The beauty of the brain's plasticity is that we can continually evolve and improve. Even the smallest step towards overcoming our limitations can carve new neural pathways, impacting our personal and professional lives profoundly.

Summarily, the rags to riches journey isn't found in mere material gains. It's embedded in the moments of doubt we conquer, the resilience we muster, the improvements we make, and the seemingly insurmountable barriers we overcome. Ultimately, it's about the journey of continually leveraging the power of neural transformation to become the best version of ourselves.

To embrace this transformation, remember the stories of those who have made the leap. Keep in mind that the power of the brain is within, waiting to be tapped. Believe in the brain's plasticity, trust in your abilities, and fuel your thoughts with positivity. Developing fruitful habits and fostering a growth mindset can be the springboard to your rags to riches story.

The power of neural transformation is in your hands. By harnessing it, you can script a tale of success that transcends societal definitions, proving that 'riches' are, indeed, in the realm of the mind.

Overcoming Adversity: Stories of Resilience and Triumph

Resilience is a vital characteristic that can greatly influence our ability to succeed. It harnesses the ability to bounce back from adversity, to endure hardship, and not just survive, but thrive. As we continue in our journey of understanding neurosuccess, let's delve into some powerful stories of resilience and triumph.

Imagine a child, growing up in extreme poverty, with scant resources or opportunities. Despite the odds, she nurtures a dream of becoming a renowned scientist. Many times she's told that it's an outrageous ambition, well beyond her reach. Despite these discouragements, she stays steadfast to her goal, and displays an uncanny degree of resilience. Unyielding in her ambition, she masters the art of doing more with less, representing the real power of determination and resilience. Today, she stands as a successful neuroscientist, and her story can provide a real-life illustration of resilience in our understanding of neurosuccess.

Another tale of resilience and triumph comes from the world of sports. Picture an athlete, who despite losing his leg in an accident, refuses to give up on his passion. Fueled by an undying spirit and unprecedented resilience, he bounces back, becoming a successful Paralympic champion. His story is testament to the fact that the mind can triumph even when faced with overwhelming physical adversity. This is the power of resilience.

These stories, while remarkable and extraordinary, are not rare or isolated incidents. There are countless more narratives where individuals, faced with adversities and challenges, have shown remarkable resilience, leveraged their mindset and brain power, and achieved their goals.

It's important that we understand, adversity doesn't discriminate, and hardships strike everyone. The crucial factor is how we respond to them. How our brains react and adapt to situations of adversity can be a defining factor in our journey towards success.

Resilience is not an inborn trait. It is something that we can cultivate and refine over time. The brain's ability to rewire itself, or its plasticity, plays an integral role in developing resilience. It's not about having a steel armor against adversity but about learning to bounce back, and bouncing back stronger.

The concept of Posttraumatic Growth (PTG) explores how people can grow and transform through the pain of their adversities. It's a shift in mindset that transforms the narrative from 'Adversity as a setback' to 'Adversity as a setup for a comeback'. This shift in perspective, this resilience, can be key to achieving neurosuccess.

However, cultivating resilience isn't about suppressing emotions or ignoring the pain. It's more about acceptance. Acknowledging the pain, understanding that it's okay to be not okay, and giving yourself the grace to heal and grow through the challenging times.

Emotions are powerful. They add depth to our life experiences. Emotional resilience is thus, the ability to navigate through a sea of emotions, not getting swept away by the currents of emotional distress but learning how to swim against the tide.

Building resilience, just like any other skill, requires practice. It involves exercising self-compassion, fostering a positive outlook, developing problem-solving skills, establishing enjoyable routines, and nurturing supportive relationships, among other tools. All these elements contribute to reinforcing neural pathways and cultivating a resilient mindset.

A myriad of scientific research indicates that adversity can lead to growth, strength, and positive transformation, essentially augmenting resilience. Adversities can be viewed as opportunities for learning and growth, thereby changing our neural circuitry for the better.

Both resilience and adversity clearly have profound roles in shaping our brain's responses and modifying our mindset, thus impacting our journey towards neurosuccess. The key takeaway from these stories lies not in the adversities faced but in the resilience displayed. Strategies to harness this resilience can significantly impact our pathways towards achieving neurosuccess.

As we move ahead in our exploration of neurosuccess, let's carry these inspiring anecdotes with us. They are not just standalone tales of courage and resilience, but an invitation to all of us to embrace adversity as a step towards growth and success.

Let's remember that challenges and adversities are often the stepping stones to success. It's through adversity that new pathways open up. It's through resilience that we cultivate an ability to see obstacles not as stop signs but as detours to something better. So, the next time adversity hits us, let's choose to respond with resilience and let's choose neurosuccess!

Chapter 12: Moving Forward: Creating Your Personalized NeuroSuccess Plan

At this far into our journey, you've gained a comprehensive understanding of the neuroscience behind success and the tools and principles that can lead to a transformative shift in your mind. Now, it's time to chart a course that's uniquely yours - your Personalized NeuroSuccess Plan. To start, evaluate your current neural health and success levels, giving due consideration to your thoughts, feelings, and behaviors. Establish a baseline – it's essential! With this, set realistic but challenging goals in alignment with your vision of success. Make a commitment to changing entrenched patterns, adopting new habits, and fostering emotional intelligence. The next critical step is deciding how you'll measure progress. Remember, the change in neuroscience is gradual, so don't just focus on the end goal. Celebrate small victories, milestones that reflect your consistency and growth. These markers empower you to see and appreciate your journey's trajectory, preparing you for a lifetime of NeuroSuccess.

Assessing Your Current Neural Health and Success Levels

In our journey to becoming better versions of ourselves, we need to understand where we currently stand. It's similar to starting a journey: you need to know your starting point to create the map to your destination. Just as you would screen your physical health before embarking on a fitness journey, evaluating your brain's current health and the success level is essential in the path towards NeuroSuccess.

Your brain's health is crucial as it affects every aspect of your life—from your ability to learn, remember, focus, create habits, to your emotional stabilities. It's your control center. When assessing your neural health, consider aspects like memory, attention, mood, sleep, and flexibility in learning new skills.

Start by assessing your memory. Are you often forgetful? Do you struggle to recall names, faces, or facts? If you're having difficulty with memory, note it down. It's an aspect you can improve on.

Next, consider your attention span. Can you focus on a task or are you easily distracted? Do you find it hard to stick to one task without constantly drifting from one idea to another? If you're struggling with attention, it's another area to focus on improving.

Investigate your mood patterns. Are you frequently anxious, depressed, or overly stressed? Are you generally in good spirits? Your moods can indicate your brain's well-being and offer insights into possible chemical imbalances or neural pathways that might need recalibration.

How about your sleep patterns? Do you have good quality sleep? Or are you plagued by insomnia, frequent wake-ups, or restlessness? Regular, good-quality sleep is crucial for cognitive functioning and overall brain health. If you're facing sleep issues, consider it another area of focus.

Last but not least, consider your brain's flexibility. Do you adapt well to new tasks and situations? Are you open to new experiences? Your brain's ability to adapt is a powerful indicator of its health.

Now, let's move from neural health assessment to determining your current success levels. Remember, success isn't just about your financial standing or career accolades; it's an all-encompassing evaluation of your life. It's about your happiness, relationships, personal development, fulfillment, health, and more.

Start by reflecting on your professional life. Are you satisfied with your career? Do you enjoy what you do? Stand back and evaluate your passion, job satisfaction, and career progress. Remember, it doesn't matter how much you're making—if you're not satisfied, it's a crucial area to enhance.

Let's discuss your relationships—at work, home, or in your social circle. Are they fulfilling and supportive or filled with drama and stress? Relationships heavily contribute to our overall success levels. If your relationships could use some improvements, kick that up on the list.

Assess your personal development. Are you learning new skills, gaining knowledge, or exploring your talents? Personal growth is a vital aspect of overall success, and if it's lagging, it needs attention.

Reflect on your physical health, too. A healthy body supports a healthy mind. If your physical health isn't where you want it to be, it's another key aspect of your success that calls for improvement.

NeuroSuccess is about overall success in life, and these multifaceted components contribute to it. Taking inventory of your brain health and current success levels provides you with clarity, allows you to set measurable and achievable goals, and offers a starting point from which you can track your progress. Remember, it's not about criticizing yourself but understanding your strengths and areas that need growth. This invaluable self-awareness is the first crucial step towards improvement and the journey to NeuroSuccess.

Setting Goals and Committing to Change

After assessing your current neural health and success levels in the previous section, it's time to dive into setting goals and committing to change. The beauty of our brains is their capacity for adaptation and growth. However, in order to ignite this growth, you must set proper goals and be ready to commit to the process.

Setting goals shouldn't just be about creating a list of all the things you want to achieve. This often leads to an overwhelming sense of pressure and can cause more harm than good. Instead, the art of effective goal setting embraces clarity, attainability, and specificity. Properly defined goals provide a roadmap to success and allow us to simplify the journey into tangible steps.

Start by crafting a vision for what you want your success to look like. Envision it so clearly that you can almost touch it, and then delve into the specific steps needed to get there. Every achievement can be broken down into bite-sized pieces, and these are the goals you need to set: attainable, measurable, and within a concise timeframe. This can include smaller daily goals, weekly objectives, and longer-term milestones.

Committing to change is the next step, and perhaps the most daunting. You're not only promising to achieve your goals, you're promising to alter your habits, actions, and perhaps even your thought patterns. It's crucial to remember that change doesn't happen overnight. Even small shifts require a commitment to maintaining the new thought processes and actions.

Let's illustrate this abstract concept with some practical examples. Imagine your ultimate goal is to enhance your productive capability, you could set smaller goals such as limiting your usage of social media during work hours, waking up earlier to make use of quiet mornings, or even learning a new productivity method. These goals are specific, attainable, and have an adoptable timeframe.

Committing to these changes will undeniably involve moments of discomfort. Waking up earlier may be daunting for a night owl, limiting social media means learning to navigate possible FOMO, and learning a new productivity method means wrestling with unfamiliar territory. However, these are the steps that spark neural adaptation and shift your brain closer to the optimized version that we're aiming for.

Right about now, you're probably wondering how to keep yourself accountable during this process. One effective tool for measurable change is journaling. Documenting your thoughts, challenges and triumphs allows you to keep track of your progress and strengthens your commitment. This method serves as a constant reminder of your resolve and keeps the bigger picture in focus.

Another tool to hold yourself accountable is through creating a support system. Share your goals and commitments with trusted friends, mentors, or even on social platforms if you're comfortable with that. Letting others in on your journey provides external accountability and can significantly propel you toward your goals.

The role of setbacks in your journey deserves a mention here as well. As much as we would love to stride unwaveringly toward our goals without stumbling, that's often not the case. Setbacks will occur, and embracing them as learning opportunities instead of roadblocks is key to maintaining a healthy mindset.

At the end of the day, remember that these commitments are not rigid shackles, but guidelines meant to assist you. There may be moments where adjustments are needed according to your unique circumstances, and that's perfectly okay. The most effective journey to success is one that embraces flexibility and resilience.

To wrap this up, setting goals and committing to change is a significant component in your path to NeuroSuccess. By embracing clear, measurable objectives, and committing to adapt your behaviors and mindset, you create substantial shifts in your neural pathways that lead to achievement and enrichment.

As we progress through our journey, we'll continue to explore tools and strategies to reinforce these commitments, measure the progress, and celebrate the milestones achieved. The journey may be challenging, but every stumble and victory will shape us into more resilient, adaptable, and successful individuals.

We've now set the stage for transformative change. Let's dive into measuring progress and celebrating milestones in the next section.

Measuring Progress and Celebrating Milestones

The journey to rewiring your brain and redefining success is a marathon, not a sprint. It involves multiple steps and stages, which should all be considered and celebrated. Measuring progress is not about singling out the lack of it, but acknowledging how far you've come along the way, and celebrating milestones that underline your growth. After all, they act as stepping stones leading you to accomplishing your ultimate goals.

It is crucial to start by defining what successful progress means to you. It's not necessarily about meeting a particular goal within a specific timeframe. Genuine progress could be as simple as recognizing problematic default behaviors, reducing instances of procrastination, or building your self-belief gradually. Look beyond the material rewards and focus on the intangibles that truly influence your quality of life – confidence, emotional stability, resilience, relationships, and intrinsic satisfaction.

Design quantitative measures of progress for your mental rewiring journey. This involves associating your progress with quantifiable data. For instance, if your goal is to reduce procrastination, you might count the number of tasks you have been postponing each week and aim to see this number gradually decline. Similarly, if your focus is on improving emotional resilience, your metric might involve logging how you emotionally reacted to challenging situations and tracking any changes over time.

Similarly, qualitative measures also hold significance. While quantitative measures provide data, qualitative measures offer insight into how you have grown as a person during your journey to NeuroSuccess. Journalling about your experiences, insights, hurdles, and victories can be one such measure. This activity helps in documenting your journey and recognizing patterns, breakthroughs, and obstacles that might otherwise go unnoticed.

Once you have identified your measures, it is vital to regularly review your progress. Creating a schedule or plan to check-in with your metrics can ensure you stay committed to the process. This could involve setting aside a few minutes every evening, developing weekly summaries, or scheduling monthly reviews. The key is to choose an approach that best fits your lifestyle and preferences and stick to it.

Importantly, every review should not just focus on what could have gone better, but also on the victories and the improvements, however small they might seem. Shifting your focus on improvements may result in a more positive experience and encourage a growth mindset. Recognize every little breakthrough, achievement, or positive change as a win. Expressing gratitude towards yourself for these wins can significantly impact your brain's rewiring process.

Remember to break your journey down into manageable chunks. Milestones are a great way to stay motivated and focused, giving you something to aim for and celebrate once achieved. These milestones should be realistic and measurable, perhaps even time-bound, but remember they are indeed yours. What others might consider as trivial might be a significant milestone for you, so avoid drawing comparisons.

When you meet these wins or milestones, it's crucial to celebrate them. Celebrations act as an instantaneous reward system providing your brain with positive reinforcement. This reinforcement, especially when repeated over time, may reinforce the neural pathways encouraging the desired behaviors.

How to celebrate? It is entirely your choice. It could be as simple as a pat on the back, a favorite meal, or time spent doing something you love. The goal is to associate the act of achieving your milestones with positive experiences compelling your brain to repeat the beneficial behaviors that led to the celebration.

While celebrating the wins, don't forget to embrace the journey with its ups and downs. There may be setbacks along the way, and that's perfectly fine. A setback doesn't mean failure; instead, it signifies growth. Mistakes are nothing but opportunities for learning that add new layers to your experience, often making your future endeavors more informed and resilient.

Recognizing personal growth and celebrating your milestones leads to a greater sense of achievement and satisfaction. It triggers feelings of pleasure and positivity, further enhancing motivation and fostering the commitment to continue with your transformative journey. It makes the long trek towards reaching your ultimate goals feel less daunting, more manageable.

The journey to NeuroSuccess is deeply personal and unique. It's not a competitive race but a path of self-exploration and development. Patience, persistence, and positivity are key, along with the time-to-time celebration of your progress. So, take a moment today to acknowledge how far you've come, even if you're still at the beginning of your journey.

Your journey to NeuroSuccess is constantly unfolding, and each step you take, or each effort you make, is carving you into a better version of yourself. Every time you make a positive change in your life, you're making a stride toward NeuroSuccess. Remember - measurable progress takes different forms for everyone and comes in different sizes. So be kind, patient, and most importantly, present with yourself as you journey your way to NeuroSuccess.

Conclusion

Your brain is the mastermind behind everything you do, feel, perceive, desire, and ultimately achieve. By understanding how it works and investing your energy into adopting brain-healthy habits, you position yourself at an advantage point in the race towards success. As you advance in your journey towards NeuroSuccess, remember that achievement is not merely confined to our careers and material wealth, but extends to our relationships, emotional intelligence, lifelong learning, and how we overcome adversities.

Bear in mind that we're wired to resist change, making the process uncomfortable initially. However, like training a muscle, the more we stretch and strain our neural circuits, the stronger they become. Overcoming procrastination, mastering your emotions, utilizing strategic learning, and maintaining optimum brain health, all contribute to reprogramming our neural pathways. Remember that change doesn't happen overnight. It is gradual, consistent, and requires continuous effort. Celebrating small victories along the way will serve to reinforce and consolidate these new pathways, making them stronger with time.

Finally, success isn't a destination, it's a journey. Each one of us has our definition of what success looks like. Therefore, NeuroSuccess isn't about striving to meet anyone else's standards but about becoming the best version of you. As you continue to journey towards achieving NeuroSuccess, embrace lifelong learning and curiosity as your allies. Gather experiences, broaden perspectives, grow, and evolve. And in this everlasting process, continue to redefine success and envision it in ever-changing glorious forms.

The Journey Ahead: Embracing Lifelong NeuroSuccess

As we reflect upon what's been explored so far, it becomes clear that our brains are not static entities, but dynamic machines capable of significant transformation. They can adapt and stretch beyond existing capacity by focusing on serious brain-training regimens combined with consistency, perseverance, and patience. Embracing lifelong NeuroSuccess isn't merely a fleeting decision, but rather a conscious commitment to stepping into the realm of continuous and optimized self-growth.

Tackling challenges with a positive mindset matters more than we may think. It's absolutely critical in nudging our brains toward growth and elongating our strides on the path of success. It isn't always an easy pursuit, but every effort counts, as the scope and frequency you choose to challenge yourself can dramatically increase your brain's strength, generating desirable outcomes.

Overcoming internal and external distractions, Fear, Doubt, and Procrastination, becomes easier with time as we learn, adapt, and grow. Refinement of emotional intelligence contributes significantly, equipping us with tools and methods to better modulate our reactions, ensuring they work for us rather than against us. The science behind these facts is irrefutable and harnessing it can unlock the gateways to profound transformation and success.

Your journey will require cultivating and nurturing habits that lead to long-term success. Remember, neural reprogramming isn't about quick fixes or temporary relief. Be patient with yourself in the process, relish small wins, and celebrate every milestone on your journey to lifelong NeuroSuccess.

Visualizations, affirmations, mindfulness, and meditations are not only brain-boosting techniques to clear your thinking. Practiced consistently, these also enable the rewiring of your neural paths leading to lasting change. They cultivate an atmosphere conducive to the formation of new, empowering beliefs that fuel progress in the direction of your dreams.

In this journey towards NeuroSuccess, never underestimate the roles diet, exercise, and sleep play. They are critical cornerstones upon which your brain health ascends to an optimized level. They're not only vital for your longevity, but are also essential aspects to excel in any endeavor you undertake.

Realize the importance of expanding beyond your comfort zone. This could mean forming powerful relationships and strong networks, which can help ensure your success. Cultivate a nature of empathy and compassion, while also learning to handle conflict effectively. You'll find these skills just as vital as any other business acumen or technical expertise you might possess.

At the heart of NeuroSuccess is the principle of lifelong learning. Continual growth, cognitive expansion, and the pursuit of knowledge correlate with higher levels of success. It extends beyond the conventional schooling system, urging you to keep feeding your brain valuable insights and meaningful lessons relentlessly. The more you engage in learning, the sharper you'll become at crafting the life you envision.

No journey is free from adversity, failures, or setbacks. However, it's the ability to bounce back that will separate you from others. Embrace resilience as an essential tool to keep moving forward, using every setback as a springboard to leap towards success.

Your journey to NeuroSuccess requires commitment. Staying brave in the face of adversity, harnessing your personal mastery, and consistently nurturing your brain health is paramount. In fact, these very commitments form the bedrock of lifelong NeuroSuccess.

Even if it's intimidating now, remember, the ultimate aim is not perfection but growth. Missteps and mistakes are part of this journey, and they serve to better shape your path ahead. They're often the greatest lessons en route to the highest form of success: growth and self-realization.

Finally, as you embark on this adventure, accept that every person's journey to NeuroSuccess is different. What works for you may not work for someone else, just as their path may not suit you. Be patient with yourself, and remember that any movement forward, however small, is progress. Embrace your journey, and never cease your pursuit of NeuroSuccess.

To conclude, the journey ahead calls for nothing less than whole-hearted commitment and continuous effort. But even more importantly, it's about embracing the essence of lifelong NeuroSuccess, for it's not just about reaching a destination, but also about relishing the joy of the journey. Equipped with the knowledge you've gained, it's your turn to step boldly onto the path of NeuroSuccess, thus sculpting the life you've always envisioned.

Remember, it's a journey, not a destination. Embrace NeuroSuccess, commit to your growth, and watch your world change before your eyes.

Appendix A: Recommended Books and Resources

In our journey to understand the capabilities of our brain, books are indispensable resources. They can provide information, insights, and practical approaches to enhancing our cognitive abilities and directing them towards success. The following is a selection of recommended books that delve into the human brain, neuroscience, success, personal development, and cognitive manipulation.

1. "The Power of Now" by Eckhart Tolle

This ground-breaking book emphasizes the importance of living in the present moment and preaches how doing so can lead to a happier, successful, and fulfilled life. By silencing our brain's chatter, we immerse ourselves fully into the present, leading to more focused and productive thinking.

2. "Thinking, Fast and Slow" by Daniel Kahneman

This book delves into the two systems in our brain that affect how we think - the intuitive, quick, and emotional 'Fast' system and the deliberate, slow, and logical 'Slow' system. Kahneman's exploration helps us understand how our thoughts and decisions are shaped, and how we can control and direct them towards our goals.

3. "Mindset: The New Psychology of Success" by Carol S. Dweck

Dweck presents an insightful analysis of how our mindset influences our personal and professional lives. She focuses on the power of the "growth mindset" and its profound impact on how we perceive challenges, obstacles, criticism, and success. It is an invaluable guide for shifting mindset towards a path of continuous growth and success.

4. "Predictably Irrational" by Dan Ariely

Ariely's book provides thought-provoking insights into why people make irrational decisions. It explores the hidden forces that shape our decisions, showing that we are not always as rational as we believe. Understanding these tendencies can help us manage our cognitive biases and make better decisions.

5. "Influence: The Psychology of Persuasion" by Robert Cialdini

Cialdini explains the psychology behind why people say "yes" and how to apply these concepts ethically in day-to-day interactions. This understanding of persuasion can enhance your personal and professional interactions, enabling you to influence outcomes in your favor.

6. "Emotional Intelligence" by Daniel Goleman

This revolutionary book strongly contends that emotional intelligence is as, if not more, important than IQ in achieving success. Understanding and managing emotions, empathizing with others, and maintaining social relationships are skills that can dramatically enhance personal growth.

7. "Atomic Habits" by James Clear

Clear's book underscores the importance of habits in our life. He shares practical strategies for forming good habits, breaking bad ones, and mastering the tiny behaviors that lead to significant results. This is a must-read for those looking to rewire their brain towards success.

8. "Nudge: Improving Decisions About Health, Wealth, and Happiness" by Richard H. Thaler and Cass R. Sunstein

This insightful book introduces the concept of "nudge theory," a groundbreaking idea in behavioral economics and psychology. It shows how the smallest 'nudges' can significantly influence our decision making, and hence our lives, for the better.

9. "Getting Things Done: The Art of Stress-Free Productivity" by David Allen

Allen provides an effective and widely acclaimed methodology for managing work and reducing stress. By applying this methodology, you can train your brain to be more productive, organized, and goal-oriented.

10. "Grit: The Power of Passion and Perseverance" by Angela Duckworth

Duckworth provides fascinating findings about the outstanding importance of grit – a blend of passion and perseverance – over talent or IQ in achieving success. The principles forwarded in this book are highly valuable in cultivating resilience and determination to achieve NeuroSuccess.

These books provide remarkable insights into understanding the brain's functioning and directing it towards success. They vary in focus but dovetail in purpose: guiding us to control our thoughts, emotions, and actions to foster personal and professional growth. However, books alone can't facilitate change. The onus of implementing the knowledge lies on us.

Alongside reading, seek out other resources like seminars, courses, and credible online platforms to deepen your understanding and application of neuroscience for success.

Appendix B: NeuroSuccess Exercises and Practices

In this appendix, you will discover engaging exercises and practices to enjoy, as you embark on your journey towards NeuroSuccess. Each exercise has been carefully designed to harness your brain's incredible power, helping you reach new heights of personal and professional success.

Exercise 1: Morning Visualization

As soon as you wake up each morning, spend about five minutes visualizing your day ahead. This mental rehearsal primes your brain to 'expect' the outcomes you visualize, effectively tuning your neural network for success. Picture your goals vividly, involving all your senses. Take note of the environment, the people involved, specifically how achieving the goal makes you feel.

Exercise 2: Mindfulness Practice

Set aside 10 to 15 minutes a day to practice mindfulness. Find a quiet space, make yourself comfortable, close your eyes, and bring your focus to your breathing. If your mind wanders, gently guide it back to the rhythm of your breath. This exercise helps clear the mind and fosters calmness, aiding in more rational thought and decision-making processes.

Exercise 3: Positive Affirmations

Choose an affirmation that resonates with your aspirations. It could be something like, "I am capable and prepared to succeed." Aim to repeat your affirmation aloud in front of a mirror at least twice a day – ideally first thing in the morning and just before sleeping. This practice retrains neural circuits, promoting self-confidence and a positive outlook.

Exercise 4: Emotional Journaling

Keep a journal to explore your emotions on a deeper level. Particularly on days when you're feeling low or stressed, write about your emotions without judgment. This exercise can provide clarity, release stored negative feelings, and enhance emotional regulation.

Exercise 5: Building Habits through Repetition

Identify a habit that you would like to develop. Commit to practicing this habit daily for at least a month, the approximate time it takes to rewire neural circuits to form a habit. Stay consistent and remind yourself of the benefits this habit will bring to your life.

Exercise 6: The Memory Palace

This mnemonic device involves associating pieces of information you need to remember with specific physical locations. Choose a familiar place (such as your house), and 'place' the information within different locations. Navigate through these locations in your mind to retrieve the information.

Exercise 7: Empathy Cultivation

Each day, try to empathize with someone's situation or feelings. It could be a friend, family member, or even a character in a book or movie. Empathy builds essential neural connections related to relational success and emotional intelligence.

Exercise 8: Neuro Nutrition

Keep a diet diary for a week, noting down all meals, snacks, and drinks you consume. Review your entries and identify areas where you could incorporate more brain-healthy foods, such as fatty fish, blueberries, turmeric, broccoli, or pumpkin seeds.

Exercise 9: Physical Activity

Engage in at least 30 minutes of moderate-intensity physical activity every day. Regular exercise promotes neurogenesis – the birth of new neurons, and boosts mood and cognitive function. Choose an activity you enjoy to increase adherence.

Exercise 10: Optimal Sleep Patterns

Monitor your sleep patterns for a week, trying to identify any irregularities or issues that could be hindering brain health. Improved sleep quality not only boosts cognitive function but also aids emotional regulation, decision-making, and learning.

Remember, NeuroSuccess is a journey, not a destination. While these exercises have been designed to set you on the right path, it's essential to maintain consistency and stay patient with your progress. It's not about speed, but longevity and sustained growth. As you incorporate these exercises into your daily routine, you move a step closer to realizing your true potential for success and well-being.

Appendix C: Glossary of Terms

Below, you'll find a glossary of specific terms, referenced throughout the book, that are linked to the concept of NeuroSuccess.

Neurons

Neurons are the basic working units of the brain, responsible for receiving, processing, and transmitting information via electrical and chemical signals. Their unique structure allows complex interconnections that form the basis of cognitive processes.

Brain's Plasticity

Brain's Plasticity, also known as neuroplasticity, is the brain's ability to reorganize and form new neural pathways in response to learning, experience or injury. This trait is key in the process of adapting to new situations and overcoming challenges.

Mindset

The term mindset refers to a person's attitudes, beliefs or perception of the world, which can influence how a person interacts with their surroundings, makes choices, and reacts to different situations. A growth mindset, in particular, is seen as crucial to achieving NeuroSuccess.

Belief Systems

These are deeply held personal and cultural perceptions and assumptions that guide our understanding of the world and our place in it. They significantly impact our thoughts, behaviors, and ultimate life outcomes.

Procrastination

Procrastination is a form of self-imposed delay or avoidance, usually related to a specific task or decision. It operates as a barrier to action, often hindering progress towards goals and success.

Visualization

Visualization involves consciously creating images in your mind. It can stimulate the brain in a way that enhances learning, skill acquisition, and goal achievement by creating neural pathways that facilitate the physical or mental actions visualized.

Mindfulness

Mindfulness refers to the act of being present in the moment, fully aware of one's inner and outer experiences without judgement. It's a form of meditation that is touted for its benefits in stress reduction and improved cognitive function.

Emotional Intelligence

Emotional Intelligence (EI) is the ability to identify, manage, and use our own emotions in positive ways to communicate effectively, empathize with others and overcome challenges. High EI is linked to success in multiple areas of life.

Mnemonic Devices

Mnemonic devices are techniques for remembering information. An example is the Memory Palace technique, where information is associated with distinct visual images within an imagined physical structure, thereby enhancing recall.

Neural Reprogramming

Neural Reprogramming relates to the process of changing thought and behavior patterns by restructuring the brain's neural pathways. This can be achieved through various strategies and mental exercises, ultimately leading to long-term changes in behavior and thought patterns.

Nutrition for the Brain

This refers to the impact of various nutrients on brain functioning. Certain vitamins, minerals, and fats, for instance, have been found to enhance brain health and cognitive function. Eating a balanced diet rich in these nutrients can support optimal brain performance.

Mnemonic Devices

Mnemonic devices are techniques for remembering information. An example is the Memory Palace technique, where information is associated with distinct spatial or visual cues, thereby enhancing recall.

Affirmations

Affirmations are positive, specific statements that help you overcome self-sabotage, negative thoughts and help manifest the things you desire. Regular practice of affirmations alters the brain's neural pathways, making the affirmed thought a reality.

Cognitive Behavioral Strategies

These are psychological approaches that address problematic thoughts, emotions, and behaviors through systematic, goal-oriented procedures. They are widely used to support change, therapy, and in the improvement of overall mental well being.

Emotional Regulation

Emotional Regulation involves the ability to manage and respond to an emotional experience in a socially acceptable and flexible manner. It allows individuals to effectively manage stress, navigate social situations, and make informed decisions. Mastering it is a key aspect of NeuroSuccess.